Marriage as Covenant

Considering God's Design at Creation and the Contemporary Moral Consequences

John K. Tarwater

University Press of America,® Inc.
Lanham · Boulder · New York · Toronto · Oxford

4501 Forbes Boulevard
Suite 200
Lanham, Maryland 20706
UPA Acquisitions Department (301) 459-3366

PO Box 317
Oxford
OX2 9RU, UK

Printed in the United States of America
British Library Cataloging in Publication Information Available

Library of Congress Control Number: 2005935782
ISBN 0-7618-3370-6 (paperback : alk. ppr.)

∞™ The paper used in this publication meets the minimum requirements of American National Standard for Information Sciences—Permanence of Paper for Printed Library Materials, ANSI Z39.48—1984

"To Him
who loves us,
and released us from our sins by His blood,
and He has made us to be a kingdom,
priests to His God and Father;
to Him be the glory and the dominion forever and ever"
(Rev 1:5–6)

and

To Sheila,
"her worth is far above jewels"
(Prov 31:10)

Contents

Preface

The last fifteen years have witnessed an explosion of articles and books written on the covenantal nature of marriage.[1] Despite the use of common terminology, theologians and ethicists have, thus far, inconsistently interpreted and applied what it means for marriage to be a covenant. No place is this disparity more evident than in the area of divorce and remarriage. To elaborate, while some authors allow for the termination of "covenant" marriage,[2] others argue that the marriage bond is indissoluble *because* of its covenantal nature.[3] These incongruous positions on the nature of marriage partially stem from biblical scholars' inability to arrive at a consensus regarding the nature of biblical covenants.

Even more fundamental, not all theologians agree that marriage is a covenant. Therefore, in this work, I will examine the nature and meaning of marriage as an order of creation. I will focus primarily on the problem: Is there evidence in Genesis for believing God made marriage to be a covenant relationship; and if so, how must it affect the way one understands moral boundaries surrounding the marriage relationship? The thesis guiding this research is that God, at creation, designed and established marriage to be a covenant relationship, and that understanding the covenant nature of biblical marriage will shed special insight on the value and significance of moral standards God says should govern the practice of human marriage.

Examining whether God made marriage to be a covenant relationship in the creation account in Genesis is important for three reasons. First, the nature of marriage in the created order is critical because it reveals something about what God designed marriage to be before it was distorted by sin. What did God expect of Adam with respect to Eve, and what did he expect of Eve in relation to Adam? And how then has sin affected our practice of marriage as compared to God's original design? Here, the first chapters of Genesis are obviously key, but later passages referring back to the creation account are also relevant because of the way they affect proper interpretation of the Genesis account.

Second, the covenant understanding of marriage is important because it lies at the heart of feminist and homosexual attacks upon standards of sexual moral behavior taught in the church and reflected in the culture. The power of these philosophical interest groups is growing. Every mainline denomination is contending with issues regarding same-sex unions, divorce, non-monogamous sex, infidelity, and non-married parenting, and political bodies are moving to revise laws on marriage in ways that increasingly favor relationships the Bible condemns as immoral.

Third, this topic is important because it affects so many other areas of life. Marriage is a moral hub that connects with moral thinking about many sexual issues such as homosexuality, adultery, gender roles, divorce, contraception, and pro-creation. Any clarification of God's design for marriage is sure to shed light on many other related issues.

I have organized this book into six chapters. Two introductory chapters will set the stage by reviewing the state of deterioration in the culture surrounding the marriage institution and by reviewing recent scholarship regarding its nature. I aim to show how severely marriage is being attacked in contemporary culture. Examples will be drawn primarily from two arenas: American churches and United States Civil law. Consequently, these first two chapters provide the necessary background for defending the thesis that God, at creation, established marriage to be a covenant relationship.

In chapter three, I review scholarship on the meaning and nature of covenant in the Bible for the purpose of obtaining the marks of biblical covenants, especially as it relates to the marriage relationship. Key elements that define the biblical meaning of covenant will be noted, and then these elements will be examined as to how they form the basic structure in various passages that define the meaning and nature of biblical marriage.

In chapters four and five, I argue that God established marriage as a covenant relationship. In chapter four I present arguments from Genesis 1 and 2 and Malachi supporting the claim that God, at creation, designed marriage to be a covenant relationship. In chapter five, I endeavor to demonstrate that subsequent passages in Scripture dealing with marriage are consistent with this interpretation.

Finally, chapter six considers the moral implications that follow from marriage being a covenant relationship. Moral implications arising from the preceding biblical exegesis will be checked by returning to Scripture in order to verify that they align with God's revelation of moral standards relating to the practice of marriage.

As I conclude the writing of this book, I wish to give thanks to so many who have helped me and encouraged me in its writing. Various colleagues and friends and Southeastern Baptist Theological Seminary have graciously read different portions and have given helpful suggestions. Dave Jones, in particular, has demonstrated his great friendship by offering advice throughout the process and helping me to clarify my thinking with regard to marriage. Dan Heimbach, as my mentor, directed me to this topic and was instrumental in laying my foundational beliefs with regard to ethics and theology. Jennifer Gray, my secretary, helped me greatly by insuring that the manuscript conformed to the proper form.

My deepest and most sincere thanks goes to my wife and family. My wife, Sheila, has encouraged, supported, and spent countless hours praying for me, not only in this process, but for all aspects of life. I could never thank her enough for her love and faithfulness.

Lastly, I desire God be pleased and receive glory from this research. "Where I am wrong, may God be merciful, may I humbly stand corrected, and may any harm done to the church be rectified. But where the argumentation of this book is right, where it reflects God's own Word and truth, may God be pleased to bring bold and gracious reform."[4]

John Tarwater
Wake Forest, NC
July 2005

NOTES

1. David Atkinson, *To Have and to Hold: The Marriage Covenant and the Discipline of Divorce* (Grand Rapids: Eerdmans, 1979); Gary Chapman, *Covenant Marriage: Building Communication and Intimacy* (Nashville: Broadman & Holman, 2003); Gordon Hugenberger, *Marriage as Covenant: Biblical Law and Ethics as Developed from Malachi* (Grand Rapids: Baker, 1998); Laura S. Levitt, "Covenant or Contract? Marriage as Theology," *Cross Currents* 48, no. 2 (Summer 1998): 169–84; Fred Lowery, *Covenant Marriage: Staying Together for Life* (West Monroe, LA: Howard, 2002); John K. Tarwater, "The Covenantal Nature of Marriage in the Order of Creation in Genesis 1 and 2" (Ph.D. diss., Southeastern Baptist Theological Seminary, 2002); Philip Waugh, ed., *Covenant Marriage: The Experience of a Lifetime* (Nashville: Broadman & Holman, forthcoming); John Witte, *From Sacrament to Contract: Marriage, Religion, and Law in the Western Tradition* (Louisville: Westminster/John Knox, 1997); and Leslie Wayne Pope, "Marriage: A Study of the Covenant Relationship as Found in the Old Testament" (Th.M. thesis., Providence College and Seminary, 1995).

2. For example, David Atkinson writes, "Divorce dissolves the marriage 'bond' and covenant," 126; Thomas Edgar notes that marriage "covenants are not necessarily permanent," in H. Wayne House, ed. *Divorce and Remarriage:*

Four Christian Views (Downers Grove, IL: IVP, 1990), 137; Andreas Köstenberger asserts, "There is reason to believe that [marriage] covenants can be broken," in Andreas Köstenberger with David W. Jones, *God, Marriage, and Family: Rebuilding the Biblical Foundation* (Wheaton, IL: Crossway, 2004), 239, 246; see also Lowrey, *Covenant Marriage*, 102; and Hugenberger, *Marriage as a Covenant,* 83.

3. For example, Carl Laney notes, "God sees marriage as a covenant relationship (cf. Prov. 2:17). . . . God does not break covenants (cf. Lev. 26:40–45), and since divorce breaks the marriage covenant made before God, it does not meet with God's approval," in Carl Laney, *The Divorce Myth: A Biblical Examination of Divorce and Remarriage* (Minneapolis: Bethany House, 1981), 47; see also Laney's chapter in House, ed., *Divorce and Remarriage*, 18; similarly, William Heth writes, "[Marriage is] a covenant relationship modeled after God's covenant with Israel . . . . The permanence of marriage is fundamentally a theological issue, rooted in the divine-human relationship to which marriage stands as an antitype," in House, ed., *Divorce and Remarriage*, 75; note, however, that Heth later changed his view of the marriage covenant in William A. Heth, "Jesus on Divorce: How My Mind Has Changed," *The Southern Baptist Journal of Theology* 6, no. 1 (Spring 2002): 4–29; see also Tarwater, "The Covenantal Nature of Marriage," 149–75; Walter C. Kaiser expressed a similar view in a personal conversation with the authors, 18 November 2004, San Antonio, TX, 56th meeting of the Evangelical Theological Society.

4. Bruce A. Ware, *God's Lesser Glory: The Diminished God of Open Theism* (Wheaton: Crossway Books, 2000), 11.

Chapter 1

Marriage Models

Since the dawn of creation, God's good plan for marriage has been under attack. Even when theologians during the early Patristic period elevated celibacy over marriage, the institution of marriage was still honored as a gift of God. In the twentieth century, however, with the rise of special interest groups, such as homosexuals and feminists, the church is witnessing a virulent attack on the marriage institution that denies its divine origin and even questions its basic value.

Feminist author Vivian Gornick writes, "Being a housewife is an illegitimate profession . . . the choice to serve and be protected and plan towards being a family maker is a choice that shouldn't be. The heart of radical feminism is to change that."[1] Similarly, "The Declaration of Feminism" states:

> Marriage has existed for the benefit of men; and has been a legally sanctioned method of control over women. . . . Now we know it is the institution that has failed us and we must work to destroy it. The end of the institution of marriage is a necessary condition for the liberation of women. Therefore it is important for us to encourage women to leave their husbands and not to live individually with men. . . . All of history must be rewritten in terms of oppression of women. We must go back . . . to ancient female religions (like witchcraft.)[2]

Not only feminists, but homosexuals have also been working to destroy the traditional meaning of marriage. James Nelson notes many theologians are shifting their views on everything having to do with sexual relationships and marriage. Rather than ask what the Bible, the church, or tradition might require, the new trend begins with subjective impressions based on sexual experience and redefines the nature and morality of marriage to fit individual preference. [3] Homosexual theologians encourage this sort of shift claiming their experience of sexual oppression gives them crucial insight on the way human beings ought to relate toward one another.[4] As a result, these interpretive communities deny and are working to counter the influence of biblically based understanding of sexual behavior in general and of marriage in particular. Clearly marriage is the focus of much rethinking these days, and this calls for careful examination of the meaning and nature of marriage as instituted by God at creation.

Ladislas Orsy, S. J., has said, "I think the effort of historians and theologians in investigating the indissolubility of marriage or the possibility of divorce and remarriage can be misdirected. The main effort should be in investigating positively what a Christian marriage is."[5] Three decades have passed since Orsy made this observation, but his statement remains as relevant as ever. Commenting on a bill before the California legislature, *Christianity Today* noted:

> When Californians passed Proposition 22 they offered the barest definition of marriage. (It's between a man and a woman.) Such a minimalist definition may be all the state can do, but the church needs to put forward an understanding of this divine institution in all its heady fullness.[6]

In this research, I take up the challenge posed by Orsy and *Christianity Today* and will seek to examine the nature and meaning of marriage as an order of creation. The thesis guiding this text is that God, at creation, designed and established marriage to be a covenant relationship, and that understanding the covenant nature of biblical marriage will shed special insight on the value and significance of moral standards God says should govern the practice of human marriage.

In order to lay the foundation for later chapters regarding the nature of marriage, this initial chapter will summarize four models of marriage—covenantal, sacramental, non-covenantal evangelical, and contractarian—noting any strengths or weaknesses.[7] In chapter two, it will then demonstrate the relevance of the present discussion with brief reviews of the way marriage is now hardly ever treated as a covenant institution—the way God designed marriage at creation—even in the church, and of how the covenant view of marriage is all but ignored by current civil law in the United States. The guiding question for this work arises from this discussion: Are these models equally valid systems for understanding the nature and meaning of marriage? Or, is one true and the other two necessarily wrong? I will argue that God, at creation, designed marriage to be a covenant relationship, consequently rendering all other models inadequate for expressing marriage as God designed it.

During the first three centuries of the church, various individuals articulated a general, Christian understanding of biblical marriage.

Although the church was unable to speak univocally regarding this issue, it did, nonetheless, write with some degree of consistency, largely expressing a negative view of matrimony. Bailey, for example, records, "On the whole, patristic literature adopts a pessimistic view of matrimony even while it vindicates its goodness, and the Fathers argue from the parable with monotonous frequency that the wedded state produces a mere thirty-fold as compared with the sixty-fold of widowhood or the hundred-fold of virginity."[8] While thus affirming the decency and integrity of marriage, patristic writers also considered marriage tainted in comparison to the state of virginity.

Gregory of Nyssa, for instance, wrote "Our view of marriage is this; that, while the pursuit of heavenly things should be a man's first care, yet if he can use the advantages of marriage with sobriety and moderation, he need not despise this way of serving the state."[9] Indeed, Gregory contended the goodness of marriage primarily flows from its capacity to curb the sexual desires of fallen humanity.[10] But Gregory's opinion was not unique among early Christian writers. To the contrary, pages of Christian literature are replete with examples of theologians cautiously advocating marriage while simultaneously communicating unreserved praise for singleness. Accordingly, each writer exerted a degree of influence on the early church's understanding of biblical marriage.

Despite this multiplicity of voices on the subject of marriage few theologians have influenced the church's understanding of marriage more than John Calvin and Augustine.[11] Whereas Augustine's teaching on marriage shaped what came to be the sacramental view of marriage adopted later by the Catholic Church,[12] Calvin's teaching on marriage epitomizes and defends the biblical notion of marriage as a covenant relationship to which we now turn.

COVENANTAL MODEL

Calvin's views on marriage developed as his theology matured, with his early writings on marriage expressing little originality. Largely following Luther, for example, Calvin opposed the Catholic teaching that marriage is a sacrament.[13] Calvin also rejected the idea that marriage was a "necessary evil" and that celibacy represented a higher calling. Instead, Calvin insisted "Man was formed to be a social animal. Now, the human race could not exist without the woman; and, therefore, in the conjunction of human beings, that sacred bond is especially conspicuous, by which the husband and the wife are combined in one body, and one soul."[14] Far from being immoral or wicked, Calvin viewed marriage as good and holy.

As Calvin's theology matured, his teaching on marriage became increasingly original. Rather than repeating arguments from Luther, Calvin began grounding marriage in the biblical doctrine of covenant. Calvin described not only the vertical relationships between God and man, but also the horizontal relationships between husband and wife with the doctrine of covenant. "Just as God draws the elect believer into a covenant relationship with him, Calvin argued, so God draws husband and wife into a covenant relationship with each other."[15] Indeed, consider the following argument from his commentary on Malachi:

> [W]hen a marriage takes place between a man and a woman, God presides and requires a mutual pledge from both. Hence Solomon, in Proverbs ii.17, calls marriage the covenant of God, for it is superior to all human contracts. So also Malachi declares, that God is as it were the stipulator, who by his authority joins the man to the woman, and sanctions the alliance.[16]

Calvin viewed God as a third party member to all marriages, acting as guarantor of the institution.

In his teaching on marriage, Calvin linked two concepts: uses of the Law and Luther's doctrine of two kingdoms. In his *Institutes of Christian Religion*, Calvin elaborated three uses of the moral law. First, like a mirror the law makes known the sinfulness of humanity and reveals how people truly stand before God.[17] Second, Calvin described a civil use for the law: "At least by fear of punishment to restrain certain men who are untouched by any care for what is just and right unless compelled by hearing the dire threats in the law." That is, because certain individuals are not inwardly driven to do good, civil governments may use the law to "bridal" them, "holding inside the depravity that otherwise they would wantonly have indulged."[18]

Calvin described two benefits from a third use of the law. First, the law is a teacher, from which Christians can "learn more thoroughly each day the nature of the Lord's will to which they aspire, and to confirm them in the understanding of it."[19] Moreover, the law exhorts believers to do right. Calvin wrote, "The law is to the flesh like a whip to an idle and balky ass, to arouse it to work."[20] This third use of the law may be called a spiritual use.

By the civil use of the moral law, therefore, Calvin contended God maintains order and by its spiritual use, God teaches believers right from wrong and encourages them to greater holiness. Calvin's understanding of the moral law provides two tracks of marital norms for covenant marriage: "civil norms, which are common to all persons; and spiritual norms, which are distinctly Christian."[21] These two tracks split nicely the responsibilities of the church and the state. The state, Calvin contended, was to enforce the civil norms, and the church was to teach the spiritual norms. Calvin moved from viewing marriage merely as an earthly estate, as Luther taught, to teaching that marriage was a covenant with God, thus extending marriage to the heavenly kingdom as well.[22] In addition, Calvin retained the Protestant conviction that celibacy was not a higher calling than marriage. As a covenant relationship designed and instituted by God, marriage was good and holy. Calvin's instruction on marriage, therefore, mediated between his contemporary Protestant church's teaching on marriage and the Catholic Church's Sacramental model.

SACRAMENTAL MODEL

Augustine taught that sexual procreation was part of God's original order to which God gave his blessing in Gen 1:28: "Be fruitful and multiply." Because of the fall, however, he believed sexual intercourse is always tainted with sin. Hence, Augustine felt compelled to justify why Christians would ever choose marriage over celibacy. For Augustine, the only two reasons justifying Christian marriage were procreation and remedy for further sexual sin.[23] Because Augustine believed the need to procreate existed primarily for Old Testament saints and thus, no longer had the same necessity, marriage as a remedy for sexual sin remained the only valid reason for Christians to choose marriage over celibacy.

In *On the Good of Marriage*, Augustine attempted to demonstrate how marriage accomplishes a remedorial function. Augustine posited three benefits of the marriage institution: offspring, fidelity, and the sacramental bond.[24] Of these three marital goods, Augustine contended the first two help with sin. God, for example, can bring offspring from the evil of sexual desires and intercourse.[25] In fact, Augustine insisted conjugal intercourse is not in itself sin when engaged for the purpose of having children.[26]

Augustine called the second good of marriage the mutual fidelity of spouses. *Fides*—faithfulness to the marriage covenant [*pactum coniugali*]—has various facets. More than merely avoiding adulterous relationships, Augustine said couples owe each other fidelity for the sake of having children and for relieving each other's weakness.[27] Hence, the first two goods of marriage, *proles* and *fides*, serve as a remedy for sin by encouraging marriage partners to remain sexually faithful to one another within marriage and by directing one's sexual energy for the purpose of offspring.

Augustine termed the third good of marriage a sacrament. Sacrament should not be confused with one of the sacraments of the Catholic Church, although Augustine's formulation is the foundation for the Catholic Church's understanding of sacramental marriage. Augustine resisted using *sacramentum* in any univocal sense, applying it with a range of meanings. In classical usage *sacramentum* denoted a pledge or an oath, such as a military oath of allegiance, as well as the resulting obligations. Thus, "S*acramentum* could denote a bond created by an oath or a vow. . . . Marriage itself can be regarded as a *sacramentum* in the sense of a vowed bond."[28] Second, sacrament expressed the permanence of marriage, analogous to the permanence of baptism, which Augustine calls *sacramentum*. Third, Augustine considered the marriage bond a "sacred sign" (*sacramentum*) of Christ's union with the Church, due to the influence of Ephesian 5:23.

Augustine based part of his theory of marriage on the premise that marriage between Christians cannot be dissolved, which he derived from Jesus' rejection of divorce in the gospels. Augustine emphasized one who divorces and remarries commits adultery. As a result, Augustine reasoned that the original company must in some manner still be married. He did not believe divorce dissolved the marriage bond. Rather, "There remains between the partners as long as they live some conjugal thing [*quiddam coniugale*] that neither separation nor remarriage can remove. It remains, however, as a source of guilt, and not as the bond of covenant [*vinculum foederis*]."[29] Hence, marriage is a sacrament to the degree that it cannot be broken—that some residual element of the marriage always remains, despite separation between the partners.

Augustine's three goods of marriage represent the first systematic attempt to integrate a theory of biblical marriage. However, the Augustinian view of marriage is not synonymous with the sacrament of marriage, though greatly influencing it. Witte recorded that "It was not until the revolutionary upheaval of the late eleventh through the thirteenth centuries that these early biblical patristic sentiments were integrated into a systematic sacramental model of marriage."[30]

During this period, Catholic clergy sought to establish the Roman Catholic Church as a freestanding, legal and political body, refining much of its theology and law, including marriage. Consequently the Church conceived marriage "(1) as a created, natural association, subject to the laws of nature; (2) as a consensual contract, subject to the general laws of contract; and (3) as a sacrament of faith, subject to the spiritual laws of the church."[31] The Catholic Church codified its understanding of marriage at the Council of Trent (1545–1563) in the *Catechism of the Council of Trent for Parish Priests*, clearly embodying Augustine's teaching on marriage.

First, the *Catechism* affirmed the superiority of virginity over marriage. "No greater happiness can befall the faithful in this life than to have their souls distracted by no worldly cares, the unruly desires of the flesh tranquilized and restrained, and the mind fixed on the practice of piety and contemplation of heavenly things." Nevertheless, the *Catechism* recognized that marriage is a gift from God.[32]

Secondly, the *Catechism* reflected the natural, contractual, and sacramental dimensions. "When these matters have been explained, it should be taught that matrimony is to be considered from two points of view, either as a natural union, since it was not invented by man but instituted by nature; or as a Sacrament, the efficacy of which transcends the order of nature."[33] Augustine also influenced the *Catechism*'s teaching regarding the "blessings" of marriage.

Hence, the sacramental model for marriage, which was shaped by the teachings of Augustine and codified at the Council of Trent, finds its basis in the book of Ephesians. Marriage is a sacred sign of the union that exists between Christ and the church, and as a result is indissoluble.[34] Although adherents to the sacramental model understand marriage as a gift from God, they still maintain the superiority of virginity. Moreover, as a sacrament, the efficacy of marriage transcends the order. Nevertheless, the sacramental view of marriage has two problematic consequences.

First, sacralizing marriage subordinates the husband-wife relationship to the legal and ceremonial control of the church. Especially since the Protestant reformation, the church has maintained that marriage is an essentially civil *and* ecclesiastical affair—marriage is established under God's role as Creator and Universal Moral Ruler. In other words, marriage is not established under God's more limited and specific role as Head of the Church or as Savior of the Elect. Stated differently, "Christian" marriage is not just for Christians, but the sacramental view of marriage treats marriage as though it is just a "Christian" matter so that a couple must be Christian before they can be truly married.[35]

Second, sacralizing marriage also incorporates a pagan notion of marriage as being a pathway by which men and women attain spiritual life.[36] In a sacramental model, marriage becomes a way of reaching higher levels of spiritual achievement, or of grasping some larger measure of spiritual power through material experience. That is, the sacramental view treats marriage as a means of spiritual transformation.[37]

NON-COVENANTAL EVANGELICAL MODEL

Some contemporary evangelicals, although recognizing marriage as a divinely instituted and sacred relationship, do not easily fit into either the covenantal or sacramental models. Adherents to this position recognize marriage as a divine institution, characterized by permanence and fidelity. However, advocates of this position reject the sacramental model because of its pagan notion of sexuality and its sacralization of marriage. In addition, some evangelicals reject the idea of marriage as a covenant, insisting the covenantal model is too rigid, legalistic, and contrary to Scripture's presentation.

These writers, although claiming that marriage is a covenant, do not fit well with the covenantal model that will be described in this text. For example, John MacArthur, a prominent evangelical pastor, writes "Marriage is a mutual covenant, a God-ordained obligation between man and a woman to lifelong companionship."[38] MacArthur insists that every wife is a "wife by covenant."[39] Nevertheless, MacArthur contends that partners in marriage may dissolve their "covenant relationship" under certain conditions.

> The purpose of permitting divorce is to show mercy to the sinning spouse, not to condemn the innocent one to a lifetime of singleness and loneliness that would not be required if the Lord had the sinning partner executed. . . . The Lord allows divorce in order that the adulterer might have opportunity to repent rather than be put to death.[40]

Although a number of evangelicals agree with MacArthur regarding the nature of marriage and the possibility of divorce, this understanding of marriage as a covenant is not consistent with the covenantal nature of marriage presented in this text, and therefore, is considered another example of the non-covenantal evangelical model.[41] Despite a number of leading evangelicals holding to this position, the non-covenantal evangelical model should be rejected. Because God establishes marriage and acts as the guarantor of the covenant, humans are incapable of dissolving the relationship. Thus, marriage is a permanent, life-long relationship that *cannot* be broken. Second, because God established marriage as a covenant, all other models must necessarily be abandoned.

CONTRACT MODEL

By the turn of the twenty-first century, society perceived the estate of marriage quite differently than previous generations. The new model understands matrimony as a bilateral contract.[42] Far from a covenant relationship designed and upheld by God, proponents of the contractarian model believe couples form, maintain, and dissolve marriage as they see fit. Consequently, an increasing number of couples are entering marriage with antenuptial, marital, and separation contracts, allowing parties to define their own rights and duties within the marital estate and thereafter.[43]

The church and state play vastly different roles in marriage under the contemporary contract model for marriage than they did under the sacramental or covenantal paradigms. Because marriage is primarily a church matter according to the sacramental model, the church interprets and enforces marital norms. The church also plays a primary role in marriage under the covenant model, although the state oversees enforcing the laws. As a contract, however, marriage is chiefly a matter of the state. As a result, neither the church nor its Scriptures define the nature of marriage. Instead, the institution of marriage finds its basis in the changing standards of human law.

In his article, "Christian Marriage: Contract or Covenant?" Paul Palmer notes several differences between covenants and contracts.[44] First, covenants are personal unions between nations, peoples, or individuals, such as marriage, but contracts create impersonal unions. Even though persons are involved in contracts, it is not the person who is important, but rather, the service for which he was hired. Contracts are primarily economic. Moreover, contracts are enacted and witnessed by human parties, but God always enacts covenants.[45] A contract creates an assumed equal exchange of obligations and benefits, but biblical covenants assign greater responsibility to the more powerful and sufficient party.[46] Furthermore, contracts focus on securing advantages for one party over the other, as opposed to covenants which focus on how each party should care or serve the other. Whereas contracts are adversarial, covenants are other-directed, selfless, and sacrificial. Lastly, obligations in contracts are legal, but obligations in covenants are moral.

The contractarian view of marriage falls short of biblical, covenant marriage for at least four reasons. First, the contractarian model has arisen in the church only recently. Although it is possible that the church took more than two thousand years to understand fully how God designed and intended marriage, it is highly doubtful. Rather, the contractarian model appears to be a twentieth century phenomenon that corresponds to cultural forces challenging fixed biblical norms. Second, the contractarian model provides an extremely weak basis for marriage, and thus does not fit well with the high view of marriage God obviously desires. Third, by linking the security of marriage to individuals' ability to keep faithfully the terms of the contract, proponents of the contractarian model depend on a weak view of the fall. Put differently, the contract model expects sinners not to sin, a position tantamount to denying the doctrine of total depravity. Fourth, the primary reason for rejecting the contractarian view is that God designed marriage as a covenant at creation, a position subsequent chapters seek to demonstrate. Not only does marriage as a contract represent a change from how God, at creation, designed marriage, it also accounts for much of the crisis presently surrounding the marriage institution

SUMMARY

In this opening chapter, I have sought to draw attention to various models from the church's history for understanding the estate of marriage. The sacramental model, as it was described, views marriage as good, although inferior to celibacy. Even though marriage is a natural relationship, used by men and women as a remedy for sin and as an estate for being fruitful and raising children, marriage is also a sacrament, symbolizing the eternal union between Christ and the church. The Catholic Church further taught that this union could bring sanctifying grace to the couple, the church, and the community.

By contrast, the contract model for marriage views marriage solely as an earthly estate. The essential nature of marriage, according to this model, is grounded in the compact between two consenting individuals. The conditions of this contract are not set by God or the church, but rather, by the consenting individuals, and are guaranteed by the laws of the state. The church, therefore, plays no essential role in marriage according to the contract model.

Lastly, the covenant model mediates between the sacramental and contract models. Covenant marriage views matrimony as good, like the sacramental model, but not in any way inferior to celibacy, like the contract model. Moreover, the church and the state both play vital roles in covenant marriage. Because humanity is sinful, the state helps enforce civil laws that maintain a certain degree of domestic order. Hence, the state plays an important role with regard to marriage. However, because marriage was designed and instituted by God, the church also plays a significant role, encouraging believers to greater holiness. Most importantly, as a created order by God, the nature and norms of marriage were established at creation.

NOTES

1. Vivian Gornick, *New Dimensions* (October 1990): 43; quoted in Francis J. Beckwith, *Politically Correct Death* (Grand Rapids: Baker Book House Company, 1993), 175.

2. Women's Counseling Service, Minneapolis, *The Document: A Declaration of Feminism* (Minneapolis: Minnesota Historical Society, 1971), 14, 16, 22.

3. James B. Nelson, "Reuniting Sexuality and Spirituality," in *Christian Perspectives on Sexuality*, ed. Adrian Thatcher and Elizabeth Stuart (Grand Rapids: William B. Eerdmans Publishing Company, 1996), 214.

4. Ibid.

5. Paul F. Palmer, "Christian Marriage: Contract or Covenant?" *Theological Studies* 33 (December 1972): 617.

6. Dan E. Nicholas, "Vermont House Approves Civil Unions," *Christianity Today* 24 (April 2000): 23.

7. By choosing these four models, I am not suggesting these are the only four models for understanding marriage. To the contrary, I acknowledge the existence of a number of models. For example, Witte also discusses a social model and a commonwealth model, neither of which make their way into our discussion. My intention in this first chapter is not to provide an exhaustive list of marriage models, but rather, to demonstrate that marriage is now hardly every treated as a covenant, which the presence of all non-covenantal models corroborates.

8. Derrick Sherwin Bailey, *The Man-Woman Relation in Christian Thought* (London: Longmans, Green and Company, 1959), 24.

9. Gregory of Nyssa, trans. Philip Schaff and Henry Wace, vol. 5, *On Virginity*, viii, in *A Select Library of the Nicene and Post-Nicene Fathers of the Christian Church* (Buffalo: The Christian Literature Company, 1887), 353. All subsequent citations from this source will be referenced by *Select Library*.

10. Gregory of Nyssa, *On Virginity*, iii, *Select Library* 5:345.

11. For an excellent source of primary material on marriage in the early church, see David G. Hunter, *Marriage in the Early Church* (Minneapolis: Fortress Press, 1992); and Philip Lyndon Reynolds, *Marriage in the Western Church: The Christianization of Marriage During the Patristic and Early Medieval Periods* (Leiden: E. J. Brill, 1994). For example, see *Shepherd of Hermas*, 29.1; similarly, Tertullian wrote two letters: *To His wife* and *An Exhortation to Chastity*. Also, see Clement of Alexandria's *The Instructor*, Book 2; *Miscellanies 2*, 23.138; and *Miscellanies 3*, 6.45. See John Chrysostom, *Homily 20 on Ephesians*.

12. Augustine, *De bono conjugali*, CSEL 41, 187–231; PL 40, 373–396; Augustine, *De sancta virginitate*, CSEL 41, 235–302; PL 40, 397–428; Augustine, *De nuptiis et concupiscentia*, CSEL 42, 209–319; PL 44, 413–474.

13. Calvin, *Institutes* (1536), 5.68.

14. John Calvin, trans. John King, vol. 1, *Commentaries on the First Book of Moses Called Genesis* (Grand Rapid: William B. Eerdmans Publishing Company, 1948), 128–9. Also, see *Institutes* (1559), 4.19.34: "Marriage is the holiest bond that God has set among us."

15. Witte, *From Sacrament to Contract*, 95. Also, see Calvin's sermon on Eph 5:22–26: "Marriage is not a thing ordained by men. We know that God is the author of it, and that it is solemnized in his name. The Scripture says that it is a holy covenant, and therefore calls it divine." Also, in his sermon on Deut 5:18: Marriage is called a covenant with God . . . meaning that God presides over marriages."

16. John Calvin, *Commentaries on the Twelve Minor Prophets: Zechariah and Malachi*, trans. John Owen, vol. 5 (Grand Rapids: William B. Eerdmans Publishing Company, 1950), 552–3.

17. Calvin, *Institutes* (1559), 2:7.7.

18. Ibid., 2:7.10.

19. Ibid., 2:7.12.

20. Ibid.

21. Witte, *From Sacrament to Contract*, 98.

22. See ibid., 111.

23. See Reynolds, *Marriage in the Western Church*, 266.

24. Augustine, *The Good of Marriage*, 24.23, *The Works of St. Augustine*, 57.

25. Augustine, *De bono conjugali*, 3,3, *The Works of Saint Augustine*, 35: "We can say now that in that condition of being born and dying with which we are acquainted, and in which we were created, the union of man and woman is something of value . . . Marriages also have the benefit that sensual or youthful incontinence, even though it is wrong, is redirected to the honorable purpose of having children, and so out of the evil of lust sexual union in marriage achieves something good. Furthermore, parental feeling brings about a moderation in sensual desire, since it is held back and in a certain way burns more modestly."

26. Augustine, *De nuptiis et concupiscentia*, 1.13, CSEL; Augustine, On Marriage and Concupiscence, NPNF 60, 269.

27. Augustine, *De bono conjugali*, 4,4, *Works of Saint Augustine* I/9, 35. Augustine, *De bono conjugali* 6,6, *Works of Saint Augustine* I/9, 37.

28. Reynolds, *Marriage in the Western Church*, 282.

29. *De nuptiis et concupiscentia*, 1.11, CSEL 42. Also see *De bono conjugali*, 7: "Entering into the marriage contract [*foedus*] is a matter of such sacredness [*sacramenti*] that it is not annulled by that separation. While the man lives, the woman he has left commits adultery if she marries someone else, and he who left her is the cause of that wrongdoing."

30. Witte, *From Sacrament to Contract*, 22.

31. Ibid., 23.

32. *Catechism of the Council of Trent for Parish Priests*, trans. John A. McHuch and Charles J. Callan (New York: Joseph F. Wagner, 1934), 338, 343.

33. Ibid., 342, 350.

34. The Catholic Church's sacramental understanding of marriage differs from Augustine's earlier assessment. Augustine said because marriage is indissoluble, it is a sacrament. The Catholic Church says because marriage is a sacrament, it is indissoluble.

35. See Markus Barth, *Ephesians: Translation and Commentary on Chapters 4–6*. The Anchor Bible (Garden City: Doubleday and Company, 1974), 744–49. See also Luther, *Babylonian Captivity* (1520), WA, VI 550–53; *Sermon on the Mount*, WA, XXXII, 376–81; and Calvin, *Institutes*, 4:19.36.

36. For a discussion of pagan sexuality, see Daniel Heimbach, *True Sexual Morality: Recovering Biblical Standards for a Culture in Crisis* (Wheaton, IL: Crossway Books, 2004), 51–88.

37. See Markus Barth, *Ephesians*, 774–49. Also see Helmut Thielicke, *Sex*, vol. 3, in *Theological Ethics*, trans. John W. Doberstein (Philadelphia: Fortress Press, 1975; Grand Rapids: William B. Eerdmans Publishing Company, 1979), 125–144 for an excellent discussion concerning the sacramental view of marriage. Thielicke uses Luther to discuss three arguments against the sacramental model: theological argument; phenomenological argument; and exegetical argument.

38. John MacArthur, *Matthew 16–23*, The McArthur New Testament Commentary (Chicago: Moody Press, 1988), 167.

39. See Mal 2:14–16.

40. Ibid., 171.

41. Other adherents to this position include Leon Morris, *The Gospel According to Matthew* (Grand Rapids: William B. Eerdmans Publishing Company, 1992); and Stanley J. Grenz, *Sexual Ethics: An Evangelical Perspective*, 2d ed. (Dallas: Word Publishing Company, 1990; reprint, Louisville, KY: Westminster John Knox Press, 1997). Marriage as a covenant will be defined in chapter two, and the theological and moral consequences will be presented in chapter five.

42. For an example, see Alice P. Matthews and M. Gay Hubbard, *Marriage Made in Eden: A Pre-Modern Perspective for a Post-Christian World* (Grand Rapids: Baker Books, 2004), 21.

43. Witte, *From Sacrament to Contract*, 22.

44. Paul F. Palmer, "Christian Marriage: Contract or Covenant?" *Theological Studies* 33 (December 1972): 617–19.

45. Chapter five will discuss theological ramifications stemming from the nature of covenants.

46. Although "responsibility" may refer to any obligations, we mean the responsibilities that flow from leadership, rather than duty in general.

Chapter 2

Crisis in Marriage

Within the past hundred years, marriage increasingly has been viewed as a mere contract between two consenting adults. As a result, marriage is now hardly ever treated as sacred, and this failure is part of the general state of emergency into which the institution of marriage has fallen in recent years. *The World Almanac and Book of Facts 2001* records approximately 1,135,000 divorces were granted in the United States in 1998, and the number of births to non-married women continued to rise in 1998 to 32 percent, up from the 9 percent rate of 1960.[1] Marriage, undeservedly, does not receive the honor it did thirty years ago.

During the twentieth century the church has had to contend with the rising influence of special interest groups and postmodern philosophy, both of which have staged a virulent attack on the marriage institution, often denying its divine origin. Consequently, these interpretive communities deny and are working to counter the influence of a biblically-based understanding of sexual behavior in general and of marriage in particular.

Sadly, attacks upon biblical marriage are not limited to special interest groups, but include leaders in the American church and United States civil law as well. Consider first how rarely marriage is regarded as a covenant institution in the American church.[2]

IN THE AMERICAN CHURCH

In recent years, the church has been littered with challenges to biblical marriage. These challenges, moreover, are not limited to any one sector of the church, but seem to have infected all mainline denominations. As a result, most ecclesial bodies are operating, with regard to marriage, from a state of disorder and confusion.

At the 1996 general conference, the United Methodist Church narrowly defeated challenges to the denomination's traditional opposition to the morality of homosexuality. In a vote of 577–378, the

Methodist church maintained its ban on performing gay unions.[3] Although the denomination successfully defeated opposition to the body's traditional stance, nearly forty percent of those attending the conference voted in favor of departing from the established teaching of the church regarding homosexuality and marriage. Thus, nearly half of the participants supported performing same-sex unions and broader participation in the church by homosexuals.

In a separate vote, the UMC's Judicial Council declared "the denomination's prohibition against performing gay unions, as spelled out in its *Social Principles*, is tantamount to church law—and not simply a guideline, as had been argued by gay-rights supporters."[4] The council promised to bring before the church courts and to charge with disobedience those pastors who presided over same-sex unions. Shortly after the council's decision, two pastors challenged the denomination's position regarding marriage and gay unions: Gregory Dell and Jimmy Creech.

Jimmy Creech, former pastor of First United Methodist Church in Omaha, Nebraska, was acquitted of performing a union ceremony for two women the previous fall. Creech and his supporters had argued the *Social Principles* do not carry the same weight as church law, but rather are guidelines. The *Book of Discipline*, they argued, is the church's law. Likewise, Gregory Dell, who was pastor of Broadway United Methodist Church in Chicago and coordinator of In All Things Charity, a movement within the church that supports same-sex unions, said that the council's decision to ban gay unions undermines pastoral authority: "It serves notice to every pastor that the *Social Principles* now become the law of the church. This is a real attempt by the church to limit the liturgical power of the pastor for which the pastor was ordained."[5]

Similarly, Morris Floyd, a spokesperson for Affirmation and CORNET (Covenant Relationships Network), asserted the council's decision to regard the *Social Principles* as church law is "another illustration of the problem of losing sight of biblical commandments for justice and love."[6] In other words, according to Floyd and Dell, upholding the church's traditional understanding of marriage as a covenant relationship between one man and one woman was tantamount to denying justice and love to homosexuals and abandoning the scriptural authority reserved for the pastor.

Unfortunately, Floyd's position is not an isolated view within the church. Jeanne Knepper, a Methodist pastor from Portland, Oregon and a spokesperson for Affirmation, said the bishops should support all of the *Book of Discipline*, including statements for inclusion. She voiced, "The language of the *Discipline* over and over is that the church is there for all people. Only in a few specific cases does it put conditions on the way the church is there for homosexuals."[7] Her critique of Scripture and the *Book of Discipline*, therefore, rests on the number of times homosexuality is denounced. She articulated that since homosexuality is denounced in only a "few specific cases," then its prohibition should not be maintained. Unfortunately, members of the United Methodist Church are not the only individuals who are largely ignoring the biblical view of marriage as a covenant institution between a man and a woman.

Few denominations typify the church's general move away from the traditional understanding of marriage better than an increasing number within the Episcopal Church, and in particular, Bishop John Spong. In 1984, Bishop Spong attended "A Service for the Recognition of the End of a Marriage," in which the participants, including the congregation, celebrated the dissolution of a couple's marriage.

According to Bishop Spong, all couples strive to raise their children to be responsible adults and to give them the security to live in an independent manner. However, since the world in which married couples reside is broken, ideals often go unrealized. "Visions are frequently compromised and ultimate goals, it seems, are seldom fully achieved. When we fail, the church needs to meet us in our pain, to enable us to stand even though we have fallen, and to give us courage to live, love and risk again." [8] Spong says the church should assist Christians in living life to the fullest. Sometimes, he notes, marriage serves that goal, and it is beautiful. Other times, however, marriage does not serve that goal and may even be harmful. "In such a case the church needs to accept the reality and the pain that separation and divorce bring to God's people, and to help redeem and transform that reality and that pain."[9] What is most surprising about Spong's statement is his concluding evaluation. He writes that the church can help struggling couples end difficult marriages without compromising its essential commitment to the ideal of faithful, monogamous marriage. In other words, Bishop Spong does not believe divorce compromises the essential nature of marriage. Life-long commitment, Spong maintains, is not part of the nature of biblical marriage, or at least not when it threatens the happiness of the participants.

Similar to the struggles in the Methodist denomination, Bishop Spong is not a mere aberration. Rather, he is one representative of a growing number of individuals who ignore marriage as a covenant institution. For example, commenting on Bishop Spong's divorce blessing, another Episcopalian, Carey Sloan III said, "[I]t is encouraging to see Spong's courage and pastoral concern. [Bishop

Spong is] asking the clergy to consider a new wrinkle in our ministry to those in need of a kind, perhaps softer touch by the Lord's hand. Certainly this might be thought of as part of our healing ministry to one another."[10] Hence, some view the church's shift regarding biblical marriage as courageous, softer, and therapeutic.

Whereas one may not be surprised a traditionally, liberal denomination ignores aspects of biblical marriage, one does not anticipate these actions from a conservative ecclesiastical body. Nevertheless, even a denomination typically considered to be conservative in both its theology and praxis, should not escape scrutiny; the Southern Baptist Convention is not exempt from these current battles.

For example, in 1992, two Southern Baptist churches made national press when they broke with tradition regarding the denomination's long-standing position on homosexuality: Binkley Memorial Baptist Church and Pullen Memorial Baptist Church, both in North Carolina.[11] More related to the topic of marriage, Pullen Memorial Baptist Church blessed the union of two gay men.[12] Mahan Siler, pastor of Pullen Memorial Baptist Church, stated, "We're taking a stand toward a responsible expression of sexuality. . . . It's a stand of support toward persons who want to commit to a long-term monogamous relationship."[13] In addition, Siler told *Sojourners* that the church's decision to bless a gay union was their way of addressing a growing concern among Christians for the increasing moral decay of society.[14] Siler refused to think gay men living in a sexual union was a matter of moral decay. To the contrary, he said homosexuality is a positive moral example and represents responsible sexual expression.

Despite the lofty and misguided reasons for Pullen Memorial's actions, the State Convention of North Carolina voted to expel the congregation from the Convention. Sadly, the general board's vote to expel the congregation was close, 59–28. Thus, nearly thirty percent of those voting on whether or not to allow Binkley and Pullen to remain a North Carolina Baptist Church were willing to allow them to stay.[15]

The American Baptist Convention supplies a second example from the Baptist denomination. The Theology Forum Adult Sunday School Class of First Baptist Church Redlands, California constructed a statement it believes accurately reflects the biblical understanding of human sexuality. For the most part, various church leaders in the American Baptist Convention accepted the findings of this class, confirming what was written in the document reflected what American Baptists, at least in part, believe.[16]

According to the forum, biblical authors were not familiar with the institution of marriage as it currently exists. Thus, the forum determined it is presently impossible to derive any concrete biblical ideas regarding the modern institution of marriage from Scripture. The forum argued that any attempt to draw fixed moral principles from Scripture regarding marriage treats marriage anachronistically and leads to misinformation regarding the institution.[17] The forum's belief that the Bible does not have anything concrete to say about contemporary marriage, however, did not stop the class from making bold statements regarding human sexuality. For example, consider the following opinion given regarding individuals for whom marriage is not an option:

> This leaves only the option of patronizing prostitutes or of sexual intercourse between unmarried adults. Paul recommends against patronizing prostitutes . . . and by speaking so highly of celibacy, Paul implies that in his context he would recommend against non-marital sexual intercourse. Jesus, however, seems to have nothing against sex between unmarried adults, and certainly never spoke against it. He even welcomed prostitutes among his followers. There is nothing against it in the ethics of the Hebrew Bible, except that it should not be achieved by taking advantage of the vulnerabilities of the woman. . . . Paul's arguments can be developed further and would indicate that sexual relationships must be tied up with committed relationships, whether in marriage or not. The Theology Forum finds itself in agreement with this: sexual relationships should involve commitment, perhaps even covenantal commitment, but do not require that this be a marital commitment.[18]

Hence, according to this document, which received positive responses from individuals related to the American Baptist Convention, sexual relations outside of marriage are permissible so long as the participants are committed to one another, even covenantally committed. According to the forum, therefore, an institution of covenantal commitment other than marriage exists between couples.[19]

While much of the church largely ignores marriage as a covenant institution, theological scholarship offers little comfort for a return to biblical marriage. Recent articles submit that Scripture is silent with regard to contemporary marriage and in some places corrupt:

> We cannot assume that God's mind and will come to us directly and unmediated. [It is] mediated through human consciousness, the categories of the human mind, as Kant has taught us. Even if the Biblical record is not in part corrupt and culturally shaped, our reading of it is. So it is that we are unlikely to derive unchangeable rules and norms from the Bible for specific behaviors. But this human

> situation does not prevent us from deriving general principles or even "middle axioms" from Scripture by use of tradition and experience reflected on in light of reason. It is not that traditional norms and the Church's teaching are irrelevant and unimportant; it is simply that the way in which they [fundamentalists] seek to use them is inaccurate. The task of ethical discourse is far more complex than they will admit. Nor is there a conspiracy to change the Church's teaching or to depart from Biblical truth; it is the inescapable theological task to relate the Bible and the Church's teaching to new situations unforeseen by Scripture and unprecedented in the tradition. We must ask how the Spirit is leading us to meet new situations.[20]

Hence, God in his infinite wisdom never imagined marriage as it presently exists—it is a "new situation." Since God did not address this situation in Scripture, believers must seek the Spirit's fresh leading in order to derive general principles based upon human experience.

Luke Johnson, professor of New Testament at Emory University in Atlanta, when asked about advances the church has made in understanding human marriage similarly responded:

> One thing that has been clarified for me is the importance of where one starts the discussion. If one begins, as I do, with a strong sense of God's continuing self-revelation—with the sense that God is still capable of surprises and that the church's task is to respond in obedience to how God discloses God's self—then the reading of scripture, while extremely important, is not definitive. The question of homosexuality then becomes not an exegetical one—not "What does the tradition say?"—but a hermeneutical one—"How do we balance what different authorities say?"[21]

Johnson denies God's omniscience and asserts that although Scripture is important, it does not speak definitively about sexual relationships.

Later, Johnson affirms homosexual unions, contending the church has much to learn from same-sex, "covenanted relationships."[22] He writes:

> Of all the marriages I know about, it's a lesbian marriage that is the longest lasting, most faithful, most productive, most socially active and most generous. The two partners are deeply spiritual people who find no place for themselves within the church. What I'm asking is whether the church ought to at least entertain the possibility of replicating Peter's response to the Holy Spirit being poured out on the household of Cornelius: If God has accepted them, why shouldn't we?[23]

Thus, Johnson not only believes that same-sex unions are covenant relationships, he also argues that the church should receive these homosexual relationships into the church as the gentiles were received in the first century. Lastly, Johnson bases his conclusions regarding biblical marriage on his experience, rather than judging those marriages according to Scripture. Indeed, the norm for assessing biblical marriage is experience and not the Bible.

The reason for reviewing the above vignettes regarding the church and marriage is to show that, despite variations, those who are seriously working to promote new trends in the American church regarding marriage are not only practicing marriage differently but are openly attacking the very meaning of marriage itself. A seismic shift is occurring taking the church away from the idea that marriage is meant to be a covenant and the effect is producing tragic results that should grieve those who care about the Word of God, who care about the church, and who care about preserving their own precious marriage and family relationships.

IN UNITED STATES CIVIL LAW

If the meaning of marriage is eroding in the church, it is in even greater trouble in American culture. Recently, the Alliance for Marriage, a small group of clergy and lay scholars, proposed a constitutional amendment defining marriage as "a union of a man and a woman."[24] The fact that a group of individuals felt the need to make such a proposal is evidence that the traditional practice and understanding of marriage is under siege and in danger of being completely ignored. State Legislatures continue to propose creative legislation in wake of increasing challenges to the marriage institution.

On May 5, 1993 the Hawaii Supreme Court ruled unconstitutional a law banning homosexual marriages unless the government was able to demonstrate a "compelling state interest."[25] The Supreme Court's decision followed a suit filed by three homosexuals who claimed that their privacy and equal-protection rights had been violated by the state prohibiting gay marriages.

Commenting on the court's decision, Barbara Dority, president of Humanists of Washington, executive director of the Washington Coalition Against Censorship, and co-chair of the Northwest Feminist Anti-Censorship Taskforce, said, "Securing same-sex marriage is, quite simply, another advance in the struggle to extend to all American citizens the equal right to enter into a contract with their life partner of choice."[26] According to Dority, marriage is a "basic civil right," a "civil contract between two people that provides certain rights and imposes certain obligations," and therefore, "a religious institution should not dictate who may obtain a civil marriage license from the state."[27] Thus, Dority suggests the Hawaii Supreme Court was merely defending and securing for homosexuals aspects of their basic civil rights. Dority not only claims marriage for homosexuals is a basic civil right, but it also is a mere civil relationship and hence, the church should have no authority relating to who should be able to enter it. In fact, Dority refers to those who oppose homosexual unions as "purveyors of mean-spirited ignorance and bigotry."[28]

On October 4, 1999 California Governor Gray Davis signed legislation granting same-sex couples benefits similar to those formerly given only to married couples. Moreover, the new law threatens with fines those who deny couples these benefits, even for religious reasons.[29] Two months later, on December 20, 1999, the Vermont Supreme Court ruled "gay couples are entitled to the same benefits and protection that the state provides heterosexual married couples."[30] The court ordered, however, the state's legislature must determine how the benefits and protection will be supplied, whether they will come through a system of domestic partnerships or through a formal marriage.

On March 16, 2000, the Vermont House responded to the court's decision by a vote of 76–69 to approve a plan allowing homosexual couples to be united through civil unions. Ironically, lawmakers viewed their actions as defending traditional marriage by "treating the legislation as a civil-rights issue. An amendment to the bill defines marriage as a union between one man and one woman."[31] Since Vermont's decision, more than 2,300 same-sex couples, many of them out-of-state residents, have been bound in Vermont with formal ceremonies.[32]

In response to recent attacks by state legislatures and courts upon Christian marriage, at least thirty-four states passed laws refusing to recognize same-sex unions performed in other states, such as Vermont. The federal Defense of Marriage Act, passed by Congress and signed by President Bill Clinton in 1996, assures that no state is obligated to recognize the legal status of civil unions or other same-sex partnerships granted in other states.[33] Consequently, in 1998, the Congress of Hawaii amended its state constitution refusing to recognize gay marriage, and the Hawaiian Supreme Court ruled that the matter was closed.[34] Similarly, California's Proposition 22 (The Defense of Marriage), which passed by a margin of 61–39 percent, allows California to refuse recognizing gay unions executed in other states.

Actions, therefore, both in the church and in U.S. civil law, indicate that new, societal interpretations of the covenantal bond are replacing the biblical foundation of marriage. Increasingly large numbers of churches are blessing same-sex unions and condoning divorce. And while a majority of state legislatures pass laws refusing to recognize these unions, votes are surprisingly close. With cultural statistics indicating a smaller percentage of individuals are marrying and yet, the number of single-parent households is increasing, the need for understanding marriage as God created it is imperative.

SUMMARY

After identifying the major models of marriage in chapter one, this chapter sought to demonstrate the majority of society, including the church, seldom treats marriage as God designed it, which accounts for the general state of crisis currently surrounding the institution. Furthermore, this crisis in marriage largely corresponds to society's shift from viewing marriage as an institution designed by God to understanding marriage merely as an agreement between two individuals. Therefore, in order for the church to counter the current dilemma surrounding marriage, it is imperative to discover how God, at creation, designed marriage, to which I now turn.

NOTES

1. *The World Almanac and Book of Facts 2001* (New Jersey: World Almanac Books, 2001), 871–3.
2. Marriage as a covenant institution will be defined more clearly in chapter three and following.
3. See Religion News Service, "UMC Bans Same-Sex Unions," *Christian Century* 115 (26 August 1998): 775.
4. Ibid.
5. Ibid.
6. Religion News Service, "UMC Bishops' Stance Draws Praise, Criticism," *Christian Century* 115 (20 May 1998): 521.
7. Ibid., 522.
8. John Shelby Spong, "Can the Church Bless Divorce?" *Christian Century* 101 (28 November 1984): 1127.
9. Ibid.
10. Ibid., 358. Also, for other positive remarks see ibid., 360.
11. On April 5, 1992, members of Binkley Baptist Church licensed one of its gay members, John Blevins, to the gospel ministry, an action that eventually led the North Carolina Convention to expel the Church from the State Convention only six weeks later. See "N. Carolina Baptist Convention Ousts 2 Churches on Gay Issue," *The New York Times*, 21 May 1992, A21; and Keith

Hartman, "To License a Gay Minister?" *Christian Social Action* 5 (November 1992): 31–5.

12. *NYT*, "N. Carolina Baptist Convention Ousts 2 Churches on Gay Issue," A21.

13. Religion News Service, "Homosexual Debate Hits Southern Baptists," *Christianity Today* 36 (6 April 1992): 74.

14. See Jim Rice, "Presbyterians Battle Over Call of Pastor," *Sojourners* 21 (June 1992): 32.

15. For an excellent discussion of congregational autonomy, see Timothy George, "Baptists and Gay "Marriage": SBC Limits of Congregational Autonomy," *Christianity Today* 36 (18 May 1992): 15. "The autonomy of the local church is qualified by the lordship of Jesus Christ. The idea that a congregation can believe anything it chooses, or do anything it dares, however outrageous or unbiblical, and still be considered in good standing within the wider community of faith flies in the face of both New Testament ecclesiology and free-church history. This distortion, born of modern rugged individualism, has eviscerated the corporate witness of the church."

16. For positive responses to the Forum's document, see Beverly Robers Gaventa, "Response to The Bible and Human Sexuality," *American Baptist Quarterly* 12, no. 4 (December 1993): 329–33; David M. Scholer, "Response to The Bible and Human Sexuality," *American Baptist Quarterly* 12, no. 4 (December 1993): 334–9; William R. Herzog II, "Response to The Bible and Human Sexuality," *American Baptist Quarterly* 12, no. 4 (December 1993): 340–5; and Everett W. Curry Jr., "Response to The Bible and Human Sexuality," *American Baptist Quarterly* 12, no. 4 (December 1993): 346–53.

17. See Theology Forum Adult Sunday School Class, "The Bible and Human Sexuality," *American Baptist Quarterly* 12 (December 1993): 301.

18. Ibid., 307–8.

19. Bishop John Spong also mentioned the existence of a covenant between two individuals other than marriage. He wrote regarding A Service for the Recognition of the End of Marriage: "We affirm you in the new covenant you have made: one that finds you separated but still caring for each other and wishing each other good will." Spong, "Can the Church Bless Divorce?" 1127.

20. John Gessell, "Human Sexuality (Again)," *Saint Luke's Journal of Theology* 31, no. 4 (September 1988): 245–6.

21. David Heim, "Homosexuality, Marriage, and the Church: A Conversation," *Christian Century* 115, no. 19 (1 July 1998): 644. For a discussion of God's providence, see Bruce Ware, *God's Lesser Glory: The Diminished God of Open Theism* (Wheaton: Crossway Books, 2000), 19–26. In this book, Ware responds to the arguments made by open theists that challenge God's knowledge of future events. Ware writes that views challenging God's absolute knowledge of future events affect "our overall conception of God and our broad understanding of living the Christian life."

22. See ibid., 646.

23. See ibid.

24. Kelley O. Beaucar, "Marriage-Strengthening Constitutional Amendment Proposed," *Fox News*; available from http://www.foxnews.com/story/; Internet accessed 12 July 2001.

25. Religion News Service, "Gay Marriage Ban Weakened," *Christianity Today* 37 (21 June 1993): 48.

26. Barbara Dority, "An Equal Right to Marry," *The Humanist* 56 (November 1996): 37.

27. Ibid.

28. Ibid.

29. Religious News Service, "New Laws Protect Homosexuals," *Christianity Today* 43 (15 November 1999): 17.

30. Religion News Service, "Vermont Court Allows Gay Couples Benefits," *Christian Century* 117, no. 1 (5 January 2000): 11.

31. Dan E. Nicholas, "Vermont House Approves Civil Unions," *Christianity Today* 44, no. 5 (24 April 2000): 23.

32. Beaucar, "Marriage-Strengthening Constitutional Amendment."

33. Dority, "An Equal Right to Marry" 38.

34. RNS, "Vermont Court Allows Gay Couples Benefits" 11. For more discussion on the controversy in Hawaii, see Kim Lawton, "State Lawmakers Scramble to Ban Same-Sex Marriages," *Christianity Today* 41 (3 February 1997): 84 and Julia Stronks, "Christians, Public Policy and Same-Sex Marriage: Framing the Questions Before We Shout Out the Answers," *Christian Scholar's Review* 26, no. 4 (1997): 540–62.

Chapter 3

Essential Elements and General Features of a Covenant

In order to prove that God, at creation, designed marriage to be a covenant relationship, it is necessary to determine the essential elements of a covenant. This chapter begins by exploring how various scholars have approached defining the concept of covenant, noting strengths and weaknesses in each method. After demonstrating the superiority of Gordon Hugenberger's biblical-concept approach, which includes various "senses," it will then delineate essential elements arising from the first sense. The chapter will conclude by identifying features often attending covenants found in the Bible.

APPROACHES TO DEFINING COVENANT

Over the last century, many scholars have examined the concept of covenant due in large part to the fact that the idea touches so many theological issues. For example, theologians have investigated the centrality of covenants in federal theology, their place within the Old Testament narrative, as well as the relationship between biblical covenants and the ostensibly similar treaties of the ancient Near East.[1] Yet, despite an abundance of research on the topic, scholars have failed to agree upon the exact nature of covenants—perhaps because they have not adequately delimited the subject. Given the wide-ranging use of the concept of covenant, it is unlikely that a single idea can accurately express the relationship between the various situations in which the term is employed.

This research will focus primarily on the nature of biblical covenants in which God is a participant rather than their function, thus avoiding much of the confusion plaguing earlier studies. Therefore, without delving too deeply into these disputed arenas, the present chapter will explore four popular approaches to the meaning of "covenant" in order to gain insight regarding its precise nature.[2]

Julius Wellhausen's Evolutionary Approach

Because the German theologian Julius Wellhausen significantly influenced interest and research regarding Old Testament covenants, his *Prolegomena to the History of Israel* provides an appropriate starting place for exploring the nature and meaning of term.[3] A survey of this work and his article "Israel" sheds much light on his contributions to an understanding of covenant.[4]

Wellhausen's evolutionary view of Old Testament religion significantly influenced his understanding of the concept of covenants.[5] Wellhausen argued that the picture of Israel as the covenant people of God reflected a relationship that developed late in her history largely as a result of the preaching of the great prophets and did not reflect the relationship as God first designed it. The original relationship between God and Israel, Wellhausen contended, was a natural one, like a family. He wrote:

> As for the substance of the national faith, it was summed up principally in the proposition that Jehovah is the God of Israel. But "God" was equivalent to "helper," that was the meaning of the word. "Help," assistance in all occasions of life,—that was what Israel looked for from Jehovah, not "salvation" in the theological sense. The forgiveness of sins was a matter of subordinate importance; it was involved in the "help," and was a matter not of faith but of experience. The relation between the people and God was a natural one as that of a son to father; it did not rest upon the observance of the conditions of a pact. But it was regarded as having varieties of mood. To secure and retain His favour sacrifices were useful; by them prayer and thanksgiving were seconded.[6]

The prophets, Wellhausen reasoned, set the stage for basing God's relationship with Israel on morality rather than on a familial bond. Eventually, their preaching and ethical emphases eclipsed Israel's natural relationship with God, which rested on the conviction of an indestructible tie between Yahweh and his people.[7]

> Elijah and Amos raise the Deity high above the people, sever the natural bond between them, and put in its place a relation depending on conditions, conditions of a moral character. To them Jehovah was the God of righteousness in the first place, and the God of Israel in the second place, and even that only so far as Israel came up to the righteous demands which in His grace He had revealed. . . . Thus the nature of the conditions which Jehovah required of His people came to the very front in considering His relations with them: the Torah of

> Jehovah, which originally, like all His dealings, fell under the category of divine aid, especially in the doing of justice, of divine guidance in the solution of difficult questions, was now conceived of as incorporating the demands on the fulfillment of which His attitude towards Israel entirely depended. In this way arose, from ideas which easily suggested it, but yet as an entirely new thing, the substance of the notion of a covenant or treaty.[8]

Wellhausen maintained the eighth-century prophets, including Hosea, did not use the word ברית to refer to the relationship between God and Israel. Instead, ברית derived from a different quarter. The ancient Hebrews had no "other conception of law nor any other designation for it than that of treaty. A law only obtained force by the fact of those to whom it was given binding themselves to keep it."[9] As a result, Jehovah and Israel became contracting parties—as the people sought to keep the Deuteronomic law. Accordingly, McCarthy summarized Wellhausen: "The original, crude, materialistic concept of the family of Yahweh [became] a higher religion in which morality is all."[10]

Wellhausen's *Prolegomena to the History of Israel* generated considerable scholarly interest in covenant research, uncovered various levels of complexity, and exposed a number of connections with contracts. But Wellhausen based his analyses more on Near Eastern religious and cultural studies than on researching data from the Bible itself. Indeed, Wellhausen's dependence on external sources skewed his understanding of what covenant means in the Bible and consequently, rendered his views on the nature of a biblical covenants, to a large degree, hardly more than speculative.

Philological Approach

Wellhausen's investigation of the covenant concept piqued scholarly interest on the topic, prompting a host of theologians to examine the precise nature of covenants. Whereas Wellhausen's understanding of the concept of covenant was largely influenced by a "history of religions" approach, many of the new efforts focused on philological investigations.[11] For example, J. Begrich challenged Wellhausen's evolutionary construction of the covenant concept in the Old Testament based upon etymology of the Hebrew word for covenant, ברית.[12] He concluded "that the basic and original meaning of *berit* was that of a legal union (*Rechtsgemeinschaft*) which was established by a simple act of the will on the part of the more powerful party."[13]

Biblical scholar Ludwig Koehler offered a second philological view of בְּרִית. In a journal article on "Problems in the Study of the Language of the Old Testament," Koehler suggested that בְּרִית is a feminine noun from בָּרָה, which means "to dine."[14] Accordingly, Koehler maintained that the essential idea of covenant relates to the covenant meal that often concluded covenant ceremonies. Koehler further asserted that the link to בָּרָה explains the phrase "to cut a covenant" customarily appearing in passages concerning covenants, "because one had to cut up food for the covenant meal."[15] Thus, whereas Begrich's study emphasized the legal and volitional aspects of covenant, Koehler's work stressed the meal that usually accompanied the covenant ceremony.

Moshe Weinfeld puts forward a third option, supposing the most plausible origin of בְּרִית was the Akkadian word, *biritu*, meaning "clasp," or "fetter."[16] He concluded, בְּרִית "implies first and foremost the notion of 'imposition,' 'liability,' or 'obligation,' as might be learned from the 'bond' etymology." [17] Thus, the "binding" metaphor helps explain the relationship between covenant and treaty. Weinfeld, then, viewed covenant as a legal union, even synonymous with law and commandment. He stated that the essence of the Sinai covenant rests in its "imposition of laws and obligations upon the people."[18]

The works of Begrich, Koehler, and Weinfeld typify philological contributions to understanding the nature of covenant. Although the concept of covenant may entail legal aspects, it cannot be reduced to meaning 'law.'[19] Like Wellhausen before them, Begrich, Koehler, and Weinfeld based their conclusions regarding the nature of covenant on extra-biblical material, thus distorting their perception. Therefore, similar to Wellhausen's evolutionary approach, the philological method renders an incomplete and biased view of biblical covenants.

Walther Eichrodt's Biblical-Theological Approach

With the publication of his *Theology of the Old Testament*, Walther Eichrodt brought a methodological shift to understanding the nature of a biblical covenant.[20] Whereas earlier efforts relied heavily on extra-biblical material, Eichrodt restricted his data to Scripture. In fact Eichrodt criticized two popular theological approaches to the study of the Old Testament—organizing biblical material according to dogmatic theology and organizing material according to the history of religious thought.[21] Against these two methods, Eichrodt proposed a third schema:

> It is not just a matter of describing the all-round expansion of the OT religion, or the phases through which it passed, but of determining to what extent . . . it ties up with NT revelation and is analogous to it. But this can only be done by taking a cross-section of the realm of OT thought, thus making possible both a comprehensive survey and a sifting of what is essential from what is not. In this way both the total structure of the system and the basic principles on which it rests can be exposed to view. In other words we have to undertake a systematic examination with objective classification and rational arrangement of the varied material. . . Nevertheless developmental analysis must be replaced by systematic synthesis, if we are to make more progress toward and interpretation of the outstanding religious phenomena of the OT in their deepest significance.[22]

In order for Eichrodt to organize his material around the idea of covenant and apply it to "all the divisions and strata of the Old Testament," he had to define covenant broadly. As a result, he became vulnerable to criticism.[23] Eichrodt responded to his critics:

> In the face of all objections, the 'covenant' has been retained as the central concept by which to illuminate the structural unity and the unchanging basic tendency of the message of the OT. For it is in this concept that Israel's fundamental conviction of its special relationship with God is concentrated.[24]

Eichrodt ordered his theology around the covenant concept because it established *a priori* the peculiarity of Israel's understanding of God. In this way, Eichrodt's treatment of covenant was not unique. "What was new in Eichrodt's treatement," noted Hayes and Prussner, "was the singularly conceptualized and static character he gave the idea."[25]

By defining covenant broadly and theologically, Eichrodt was able to relate various concepts in Scripture. Unlike earlier evolutionary and philological treatments, Eichrodt found the basis of his conclusions in Scripture rather than outside sources. Nevertheless, Eichrodt's biblical-theological approach has a weakness. Because he defined covenant broadly in order to apply it across all divisions of the Old Testament, and because he *a priori* considered covenant the theological center of Scripture, Eichrodt was particularly susceptible to the error of "illegitimate totality transfer."[26] Therefore, Eichrodt's biblical-theological approach, while providing various advantages to earlier approaches, also fails to define completely the precise nature of biblical covenants without succumbing to current hermeneutic conundrums.

Gordon Hugenberger's Biblical-Concept Approach

Like Eichrodt, Gordon Hugenberger also approached the meaning of covenants by restricting his attention to the biblical record. In addition to limiting his concentration to biblical covenants, Hugenberger utilized a concept oriented approach, allowing him to avoid many of the pitfalls plaguing earlier efforts.[27]

Whereas diachronic approaches explain *how* a word came to be used with a particular sense at a specific time in history, a concept oriented approach determines *what* a lexeme means at a certain time. One does not need to know the *history* of the language, or of its lexical stock, in order to understand the sense of utterances today. One way to determine the "sense" of a word is through a concept oriented approach.

Most lexemes have more than one sense.[28] For example, the word "bank" may have the following senses: a raised mass of earth; slope of a hill; and the ground beside a river. Each of these senses relate to a single lexeme. The "sense" of a word is the concept denoted by that word. Thus, the "sense" of a word, or the concept, is "a cognitive construct, a discrete bundle of meanings composing an independent unit of meaning with a central, or prominent element, further defined by other delimiting elements."[29] Consider the following illustration.

One may define the concept "bicycle" in terms of a central component—vehicle—qualified by delimiting elements—with two wheels, for one person, pedal-propelled, and having handle bars. To prove the validity of the delimiting elements, one may test them with diagnostic sentences, such as: It is a bicycle, but it has handlebars. Because the sentence is semantically anomalous, one should understand handlebars to be an essential element of bicycle. In his book, *Marriage as Covenant*, Gordon Hugenberger utilized a similar concept oriented approach to understand the meaning of covenant, and from this, Hugenberger identified six different senses of the Hebrew word בְּרִית.[30]

Hugenberger defined the predominant sense of בְּרִית in Biblical Hebrew as "an elected, as opposed to natural, relationship of obligation established under divine sanction."[31] Similarly, Mendenhall described covenant as "A solemn promise made binding by an oath, which may be either a verbal formula or symbolic action."[32] Hugenberger expressed that this sense is intended by the English word "covenant." When understood in this manner, בְּרִית may refer to three different relationships: relationships between Yahweh and his people; secular relationships; and political relationships.[33]

Since Wellhausen's initial effort, numerous works have focused on "the apparent analogy between parts of the Old Testament and Ancient Near Eastern texts. By far the most important has been the comparison with treaty texts, especially those between sovereigns and vassals."[34] Of significance for this study, not all covenants, even of the first sense, are treaties.

For instance, when "cup" is defined as a "container with a handle and used for drinking," various concepts may fit this definition, such as a mug. Not all cups, however, are mugs. So, whereas "treaty" may fit the definition of "covenant" as it is defined in the first sense, not all covenants are treaties, and therefore, not all covenants possess each of the celebrated features of ancient Near Eastern treaties. Despite Hugenberger identifying five additional senses of the Hebrew word בְּרִית, it is his first sense that impacts this study most directly.

Hugenberger recognized the broad semantic range of בְּרִית and thus, avoided the error of "illegitimate totality transfer."[35] Previous attempts to define the precise nature of "covenant" did not consistently exercise such caution. Wellhausen, Begrich, Koehler, and Eichrodt each implied that a single definition sufficiently and fully captured the idea of a biblical "covenant." Wellhausen's assertion that בְּרִית is synonymous with treaty and law falsely presumes the use of only one sense of the term. Just as not all cups are mugs, so also not all covenants are treaties.

Throughout this study, I will follow Hugenberger's definition of "covenant" in the context of Scripture for three reasons. First, Hugenberger's definition falls in line with those previously introduced by Begrich, Mendenhall, and Kline, which demonstrates that this definition lies well within the mainstream of credible scholarship regarding covenant research. Second, Hugenberger's definition arises from the biblical data itself, not from Ancient Near Eastern history, which means it is not skewed by competing theories of interpretation arising from speculative external sources with no clear relation to the Bible itself. Third, by choosing a biblical-concept, as opposed to a developmental, sociological history of religions and culture approach, Hugenberger's definition effectively transcends current hermeneutic conundrums that tend to immobilize all possible analysis and application of biblical revelation concerning the covenant nature of marriage. Because Hugenberger sufficiently defines a biblical covenant, the next section will focus on summarizing his research. Rather than analyzing and critiquing Hugenberger, we will assume the essential elements of a covenant arising from his definition and apply them in the following chapters.

ESSENTIAL ELEMENTS OF COVENANT

Using a biblical-concept approach, Hugenberger defined covenant as "an elected, as opposed to natural, relationship of obligation established under divine sanction."[36] Understood in this manner, the central component of a covenant is relationship. Moreover, he qualifies it by delimiting elements—elected, with a non-relative, involving obligations, and established through an oath. Lastly, he tests the validity of each element with four diagnostic statements, which is illustrated in the following discussion.

Personal Relationship

The first diagnostic sentence (He made a covenant, but it was with another person.) demonstrates "relationship" is essential to the nature of בְּרִית.[37] Whereas Atkinson considered "covenant" synonymous with "relationship," Hugenberger rejected this believing it was too narrowly defined. A "relationship" only expresses one aspect of the covenant concept. Biblical covenants in which God participates, however, involves considerably more then the single idea of a relationship, though this component is important. Consider, for instance, how Malachi refers to "the wife of your covenant" (2:14). If a covenant is nothing more than a relationship, then Malachi's comment says nothing at all and would make as much sense as a reference to "your female wife."

While "covenant" is certainly more than "relationship," the idea of relationship is fundamental to the understanding of covenant. Covenants in the Bible always involve two or more parties:

> The majority of the occurrences of בְּרִית in the Old Testament refer to covenants where God is one of the partners, as for example the covenants between: Yahweh and Noah (Gen. 6:18; 9:9–17), Yahweh and Abraham (Gen. 15:18–18; 17:1–4; etc), Yahweh and Abraham together with his descendants (Gen. 17:7; etc.), Yahweh and Isaac (Gen. 17:21; etc.), Yahweh and the Patriarchs (Exod. 6:4), Yahweh and Israel (Exod. 19:5; etc.), Yahweh and Phinehas (Num. 25:12f.), Yahweh and David (2 Chron. 7:18; etc.), Yahweh and Levi (Mal. 2:4ff.), Yahweh and the eschatological Israel (Jer. 31:31; Isa. 42:6; 49:6–8; 55:3; etc.), and so on.[38]

Yahweh was not always one of the parties in biblical covenants. However, even in covenants where God was not one of the covenanting parties, he still acted as guarantor of the covenant.[39]

Familial and social relationships frequently provide the model for the obligations of a covenant and for the terminology referencing the covenant partners.[40] Amos used "covenant of brothers" to refer to the relationship between Israel and Tyre (Amos 1:9). Comparably, the terms 'father' and 'son' may also designate covenanting parties, such as the covenant between God and David. Through the prophet Nathan, the Lord said to David:

> When your days are fulfilled and you rest with your fathers, I will set up your seed after you, who will come from your body, and I will establish his kingdom. He shall build a house for my name, and I will establish the throne of his kingdom forever. I will be his Father, and he shall be my son (2 Sam 7:12–14).

Similarly, referring to the remnant of Israel, Jeremiah recorded the words of the Lord: "They shall come with weeping, and with supplications I will lead them. I will cause them to walk by the rivers of waters, in a straight way in which they shall not stumble; For I am a Father to Israel, and Ephraim is my firstborn" (Jer 31:9; see also Exo 4 and Hos 11).

Alongside the terms "brother," "father," and "son," no familial relationship designates covenanting parties in Scripture more often than the husband-wife analogy. Examples abound in Isaiah, Jeremiah, Ezekiel, and most clearly in the story of Hosea and his wife. Although these instances do not prove the covenant nature of marriage, each strongly underscores the relational quality of בְּרִית.

From the social sphere, the terms "lord" and "servant" designate the parties to a covenant, as well as the terms "friend," "companion," and "partner." Each of these familial and social terms draws attention to the relational nature of covenants. Accordingly, P. Kalluveettil wrote:

> The idea, "I am yours, you are mine" underlies every covenant declaration. This implies a quasi-familial bond which makes sons and brothers. The act of accepting the other as one's own reflects the basic idea of covenant: an attempt to extend the bond of blood beyond the kinship sphere, or, in other words, to make partner one's own flesh and blood. The study of the DF [declaration formulae] has shown that covenant is relational.[41]

Hence, "relationship" is the first essential, if not central, element of biblical covenants.

With a Non-Relative

A second diagnostic statement (He made a covenant, but it was with a non-relative.) demonstrates a בְּרִית is both elected and with a non-relative. Covenants are not naturally occurring relationships, but are chosen. Frequently, covenants are cut or (re)made (כָּרַת - 63x), confirmed or established (הֵקִים - 12x), given (נָתַן - 3x), entered (בּוֹא - 3x; הֵבִיא - 1x; עָבַר - 1x), issued (שִׂים - 1x). The use of such verbs indicates that at least one party of a covenant must willfully choose to establish a covenant relationship.

Not only is a covenant an elected relationship, but it is also an affiliation that reaches beyond the familial attachments. William Heth "argued that the covenant and consummation of marriage made two totally unrelated people as closely related as they will be to their own flesh and blood children."[42] Hence, McCarthy was able to write, "There is no doubt that covenants, even treaties, were thought of as establishing a kind of quasi-familial unity."[43] Covenants, therefore, are elected relationships that extended natural ties beyond blood.[44]

Involving Obligations

A third diagnostic statement (He made a covenant, but it was one with obligations.) demonstrates obligation is an essential element of biblical covenants. Most scholars agree that covenant requires obligation. Indeed, E. Kutsch and M. Weinfeld begin with an understanding of obligation.[45] בְּרִית in many Old Testament instances functions as a commandment, such as Psalm 111:9 and Judges 2:20. In other instances בְּרִית is synonymous with law and commandment, such as Deuteronomy 4:13 and 33:9.[46] Accordingly, McCarthy wrote:

> All covenants . . . have their conditions. They must be defined somehow or other. These definitions are their conditions or stipulations which may often be assumed, things which are simply so well known in a culture that they need not be stated explicitly.[47]

That obligation is essential, as well as vitally important, may be seen in the following diagnostic question involving oaths.

Established Under Oath

The fourth diagnostic statement (He made a covenant, but it was one with an oath.) demonstrates the requisite nature of oath for covenants. "While one need not accept [the] definition of ברית as "oath," the relative indispensability of an oath for ratifying a covenant commands a widespread scholarly consensus."[48] Weinfeld noted covenants include a conditional curse: "May thus and thus happen to me if I violate the obligation."[49] The oath binds the parties. A covenant, therefore, consists of obligations accompanied by a "curse" if not fulfilled. Consequences and punishment await those who do not fulfill their part of the covenant. Thus, numerous texts closely associate "covenant" with "oath," such as Gen 26:28, Deut 29:11, and Ezek 17:13, and hence, demonstrate that an oath is an essential element for a covenant.[50] The importance of these obligations is seen, for example, in the way the LORD handles violations. Consider Israel's covenant with God inaugurated on Mount Sinai.

On Mount Sinai, the Lord established a covenant with Israel, stipulating that she be a "special treasure . . . a kingdom of priests, my holy nation" (Exod. 19:4, 6). For Israel's part, the Lord demanded obedience (Exod. 19:5). Shortly after the establishment of this covenant, however, Scripture records Israel's disobedience to the obligations of the agreement. Indeed, even while Moses was receiving the Ten Commandments—the formal record of the covenant—the people were making for themselves and worshipping false gods.[51] Sadly, this incident was not an aberration as this behavior continued throughout Israel's trek toward the promised land. Furthermore, before entering the land, Moses wrote a song predicting that the people would not be faithful to their covenant with Yahweh asserting, "I know that after my death you will become utterly corrupt" (Deut. 31:29). The book of Judges records the fulfillment of Moses' grim prophecy:

> After that generation died, another generation grew up who did not acknowledge the LORD or remember the mighty things he had done for Israel. Then the Israelites did what was evil in the LORD's sight and worshiped the images of Baal. They abandoned the LORD, the God of their ancestors, who had brought them out of Egypt. They chased after other gods, worshiping the gods of the people around them. And they angered the LORD (Judg. 2:10–13).

The fact that Israel's disobedience "angered the LORD," which eventually culminated in the captivity of the nation, provides another clue regarding the nature of covenants in which God participates. To elaborate, Israel's disobedience did not result in dissolution of her covenant with the Lord, but rather it merited divine punishment. For Israel this repeated punishment itself was an indication that her covenant with God was not dissolved, but still in effect. Indeed, Scripture is replete with examples of men breaking various covenants in which the Lord was a participant; yet, such violations never dissolved the covenants in question, they merely provoked God's wrath and censure.

Old Testament scholar Bruce Waltke notes that God uses blessings and curses to encourage obedience to the covenant. He writes, "The curses and blessings of the covenant that obliged Israel to keep YHWH's ethical demands gave Israel incentive to keep them. By these unilateral commitments, the relationship between YHWH and Israel was not contractual but covenantal—devoted and loving toward one another."[52] This recurring divine punishment is *de facto* evidence of the enduring nature of biblical covenants. Indeed, if the transgressed covenants for which God meted out punishment were not in effect at the time of divine chastisement, then the Lord's censure would be baseless and unjust. Biblical covenants, consequently, entail an elected relationship of obligations, established by an oath, and encouraged by corresponding curses and blessings.

Conclusion

By using a biblical-concept approach, Hugenberger defined covenant in terms of a central component qualified by delimiting elements, and then he tested each element of his definition by means of diagnostic statements.[53] Hugenberger defined covenant as "an elected, as opposed to natural, relationship of obligation established under divine sanction."[54] Understood in this manner, the central component—relationship—qualified by delimiting elements—elected, with non-relative, involves obligations, and established through an oath—was shown to constitute a valid definition. Therefore, using Hugenberger's definition, the essential elements of a covenant are: (1) relationship; (2) with a non-relative; (3) involves obligations; and (4) is established under oath.

GENERAL FEATURES

In addition to the essential elements present in every covenant of the first sense, various general features also characterize a number of biblical covenants. Becoming aware of these additional features will also help one recognize the existence of biblical covenants. The majority of general features issue from the essential elements of a covenant.

Covenants are Unilaterally Dependent on the Will and Authority of God

For example, because covenants of the first sense are established under divine sanction, they unilaterally depend on the will and authority of God. As a witness (עֵד) to the covenants, God becomes the guarantor of the covenant. For instance, Genesis thirty-one contains the story of Jacob leaving for the land of Canaan. After being overtaken by Laban, Jacob entered a covenant with Laban (Gen 31:44). Upon entering the covenant, Laban stated, "May the Lord watch between you and me when we are absent one from another. If you afflict my daughters, or if you take other wives besides my daughters, although no man is with us—see God is witness between you and me" (Gen 31:55). Since God was a witness to the agreements between the men, their agreement was in essence a pledge to God.[55] Each participant in the covenant swore to God to be faithful to the terms of the covenant and invoked God to respond against any breach of the covenant.[56]

Similarly, Jonathan and David entered a covenant (1 Sm 20:16). As with Jacob and Laban, Jonathan appealed to God to act against any violation of the covenant terms. "Then Jonathan said to David, 'The Lord God of Israel is witness'" (1 Sm 20:12). By identifying God as the "witness" to the covenant, both parties understood God was the one who enforced and validated its conditions. Here, God is not merely the one who punishes offenders, although he does, but more importantly, he authorizes the covenant. God is viewed, according to Scripture, as the one who guarantees the covenant stipulations.[57] Because covenants are established under divine sanction and have God as their witness, they are dependent on his will and authority.

Compliance with the Terms of the Covenant is Relevant to the Reception of Blessings and Curses

If God is witness to a covenant and guarantees its obligations are fulfilled, then it follows that compliance with the terms of the covenant is relevant. In fact, covenanting parties call upon an outside authority to impose privileges and sanctions (blessings and curses) in accordance with keeping covenant obligations.

For example, after reaffirming God's covenant with Israel and imploring the people of God to live in obedience to it, Joshua said:

> See I have set before you today, life and good, death and evil, in that I command you today to love the Lord your God, to walk in His ways, and to keep His commandments, His statutes, and His judgments, that you may live and multiply, and the Lord your God will bless you in the land which you go to possess. But if your heart turns away so that you do not hear, and are drawn away, and worship other gods and serve them, I announce to you today, you shall surely perish (Deut. 30:15–18).

In this example it is clear that Joshua related the reception of blessings (or curses) to compliance (or non-compliance) with the terms of the covenant. Indeed, God expected those who chose to enter into a covenant with him to keep the terms of the agreement.[58] Yet, note that non-compliance with the covenant obligations did not dissolve the agreement, but merely resulted in cursing for the disobedient party ("you shall surely perish"). In his book, *The Consequences of the Covenant*, George Buchanan explores this facet of covenants further, noting that in the Bible covenanters were expected to follow a prescribed pattern of life in order to remain in God's favor.[59] Indeed, Scripture equates abandoning the obligations of a covenant with turning from the way of life to the way of death (Prov. 2:18–19). Moreover, the inability of covenant partners to walk away from their covenant commitments highlights the enduring nature of such agreements.

Hence, compliance with the terms of the covenant are relevant to the reception of blessings and curses.

Covenants are Validated and Sealed by a Sign

Biblical covenants are often recognized and sealed by a 'sign.' For example, as a sign of his covenant with Noah, God gave a rainbow: "And God said, 'This is the sign of the covenant I am making between me and you and every living creature with you, a covenant for all generations to come. I have set my rainbow in the clouds, and it will be the sign of the covenant between me and the earth'" (Gen 9:12–16). Similarly, Scripture records circumcision is the "sign of the covenant" that God made with Abraham (Gen 17:11). More than a symbol, a covenant sign conveys the authority of the enacting party and expresses the covenant itself.[60]

Covenant Obligations are Life-long

Biblical covenants in which God participates are characterized by the permanent nature of their obligations—either they are binding for life or they are everlasting. Consider the words used by the biblical writers to describe the indissoluble nature of covenants. For example, Scripture often records that covenanting parties "will not forget"[61] or will "remember"[62] the covenant, indicating their lasting commitment to the terms of the agreement. Similarly, covenanting members oftentimes promise to be "faithful" to each other[63] and to "keep" the covenant,[64] even "forever."[65] While these terms seem to point toward the irrevocable nature of biblical covenants, perhaps the greatest proof of the unending nature of such agreements comes from the pen of the apostle Paul who, in an argument from the lesser to the greater, wrote that even a covenant between men—as opposed to a divinely initiated covenant—if confirmed, "cannot be annulled" (Gal. 3:15). Indeed, a survey of biblical covenants reveals that covenanting parties understood this to be true and therefore did not enter into covenants hastily. Consider, furthermore, the manner in which covenants were established.

Covenanting parties often signified a new covenant by taking blood from a sacrifice. The Lord made [כָּרַת] a covenant with Abraham by passing between the bodies of sacrificed animals (Gen 15:9-17). The covenant parties promised by the covenant ceremony that "the fate of the animals should befall him in the event he does not keep the בְּרִית."[66] Hence, God warns those who act faithlessly toward their "wife by covenant" (Mal 2:14): "Therefore, take heed of your life" (Mal 2:16). Because obligations within a covenant relationship are permanent, entrance into a covenant must not be taken lightly.[67]

Recently, a growing number of biblical scholars have begun to challenge the long-held belief in the inviolable nature of covenants—especially in regard to the covenant of marriage.[68] For example, in his book *God, Marriage, and Family: Rebuilding the Biblical Foundation*, Andreas Köstenberger writes, "There is reason to believe that some biblical covenants can be and in fact are terminated."[69] William Heth, relating how he came to change his mind regarding Scripture's position on divorce and remarriage, similarly notes "biblical covenants can be violated and dissolved."[70] Interestingly, both Köstenberger and Heth appeal to the work of Gordon Hugenberger as the basis for their belief that covenants may be dissolved. Hugenberger contends that covenants can be both violated and dissolved, asserting that these ideas are conveyed by the same Hebrew expression (Hiphil of פָּרַר + בְּרִית).[71] In order to corroborate this claim, Hugenberger cites fourteen scriptural examples of covenants that were ostensibly dissolved (Gen. 17:14; Lev. 26:44; Deut. 31:20; 1 Ki. 15:19; Isa. 33:8; 24:5; Jer. 11:10; 14:21; 31:32; 33:20; Ezek. 16:59; 17:15; 44:7; Zech. 11:10–11).[72]

Despite Hugenberger's monumental contribution to the study of biblical covenants, I am not persuaded by his evidence for dissolubility. While Hugenberger correctly notes that the Hebrew word פרר may be translated with the English term "broken" or "annulled"[73]—connoting violation or dissolution—פרר does not necessarily carry both meanings at the same time. Imposing more than one meaning simultaneously upon פרר is what James Barr calls the error of "illegitimate totality transfer."[74] In other words, it is wrong to conclude that because a covenant was "broken," it was, therefore, "dissolved." An examination of the fourteen aforementioned examples, we believe, sufficiently demonstrates this truth.

First, three of the passages (1 Ki. 15:19; Isa. 33:8; and Ezek. 17:15) cited by Hugenberger refer to treaties between men where God is clearly not a covenanting party. Thus, even if these agreements were dissolved, they would have no bearing upon this study for we are solely concerned with covenants in which God is a part. With that stated, it is not even certain that any of these three examples constitute an occasion on which a covenant was dissolved. In fact, the example from Ezekiel seems to illustrate the exact opposite as the prophet asks, "Can Israel break her sworn treaties like that and get away with it" (Ezek. 17:15)? The Lord answers with a resounding, "No!" (Ezek. 17:16). By allowing Israel to be punished, then, the Lord demonstrated the applicability and enduring nature of the terms of the covenant. Thus, these three examples fail to demonstrate that covenants in which God participates can be dissolved.

Second, two of Hugenberger's examples (Jer. 14:21; 33:20) deal with the prophet Jeremiah's consideration of whether or not the Lord will dissolve his covenant with Israel. Jeremiah records a prayer on behalf of Judah, "LORD, we confess our wickedness and that of our ancestors, too. We all have sinned against you. For the sake of your own name, LORD, do not disgrace yourself and the throne of your glory. Do not break your covenant with us" (Jer. 14:20–21). While it could be argued from this prayer that Jeremiah believed it was possible for God to dissolve his covenant, later God revealed that annulment of the covenant was not possible, not even theoretically, as he declared, "I have loved you, my people, with an everlasting love. With unfailing love I have drawn you to myself. I will rebuild you" (Jer. 31:3–4). Furthermore, in Hugenberger's second example from Jeremiah, God demonstrates the permanence of his covenant by comparing it to the times of night and day: "If you can break my covenant with the day and the night so that they do not come on their usual schedule, only then will my covenant with David, my servant, be broken" (Jer. 33:20).

Thus, these two examples fail to demonstrate that biblical covenants in which God participates can be dissolved—indeed, they seem to indicate the exact opposite.

Third, eight examples mentioned by Hugenberger (Gen. 17:14; Lev. 26:44; Deut. 31:20; Isa. 24:5; Jer. 11:10; 31:32; Ezek. 16:59; 44:7) refer to God's people violating the terms of a covenant. A careful reading of these texts, however, reveals that such violations did not dissolve the covenants in question. For example, should one believe that the Abrahamic covenant was dissolved (Gen. 17:14)? To the contrary, Scripture evidences that God's covenant with Abraham was "forever" and "eternal" (Gen. 13:15; 17:8). Moreover, on at least eight different occasions, Scripture affirms that God "remembered" his covenant with Abraham.[75] Thus, Gen. 17:14 cannot represent a dissolved covenant.

Contrary to Hugenberger's interpretation, these eight examples of Israel "breaking" their covenant with the Lord beautifully illustrate God's attitude toward the nature of covenants in which he participates. For example, Moses prophesied that the people would rebel and break God's covenant (Deut. 31:20), and Scripture repeatedly records the fulfillment of this prophecy and its subsequent consequences (Isa. 24:5; Jer. 11:10; 31:32; Ezek. 16:59; 44:7). Yet, as I have argued above, the Lord's punishment of his people for covenant violations is itself a *de facto* demonstration of the enduring nature of these arrangements. Ralph Alexander writes that the Lord's punishment of his people affirms "his immutable faithfulness to his covenants."[76] Similarly, Andersen and Freedman comment on God's wrath toward covenant disobedience noting that, "The punishment is not an expression of a broken relationship. On the contrary, it is enforced within the relationship; punishment maintains the covenant."[77] Therefore, as with the previous examples, these eight citations fail to demonstrate that biblical covenants in which God participates can be dissolved.

The prophet Zechariah presents the final example (Zech. 11:10–11) cited by Hugenberger. When Israel returned from exile, God implored the people not to act like their fathers had before them (Zech. 1:1–6), for real blessings, Zechariah records, will come only when God's people obey him and walk in righteousness (3:7; 6:15; 7:9–14; 8:14–17). Sadly, however, the people acted as did their ancestors whose behavior had caused them to be exiled (Zech. 7:1–14). The people of Zechariah's day had rejected the pleas of the righteous and consequently, writes the prophet, the Lord would withhold his covenant protection if there was no repentance (Zech. 11:10)—that is, God would "break" his covenant. Did the Lord, therefore, dissolve the covenant he had made? Certainly not, as the last three chapters of the book present an eschatological picture of God pouring out his grace upon the nation in the end times (12:10–14:11). Once again, far from dissolution, God's judgment demonstrates his faithfulness to the covenant.

In addition to the fourteen examples cited by Hugenberger, David Jones and I surveyed every example of בְּרִית in the Old Testament (267 examples), as well as of διαθήκη and συνθηκη in the New Testament (34 examples), and were unable to discover *a single example of a dissolved covenant in which God participated.* Like the language used to describe the nature of biblical covenants, the manner in which covenants are established, and the way in which God deals with covenant violations, the absence of any dissolved covenants in which God participates provides evidence that points to the indissoluble nature of biblical covenants.

The Weaker Party in a Covenant Experiences a Name Change

Biblical covenants also may be characterized by changing the name of the weaker party, indicating that one stands under a new authority and protection. After entering into a covenant relationship with Abram and Sarai, for example, God changed their names to "Abraham" and "Sarah" (Gen 17:4–5). Similarly, God changed Jacob's name to "Israel" to signal his covenant relationship with Jacob's family (Gen 32:28). Perhaps John had this in mind when he wrote: "He who overcomes I will make a pillar in the temple of my God. Never again will he leave it. I will write on him the name of my God and the name of the city of my God, the new Jerusalem, which is coming down out of heaven from my God; and I will also write on him my new name" (Rev 3:12).[78] John writes that God will give a new name and protection to those who rest in his authority.

Henri Blocher makes a similar observation in his book *In the Beginning: The Openning Chapters of Genesis.* With reference to Adam naming the animals, Blocher writes:

> Thus, he indicates the right that he has over them, as the pharaoh will show his suzerainty over his vassal by changing his name from Eliakim to Jehoiakim (2 Ki. 23:34) and Nebuchadnezzar will show his over Mattaniah whose name was changed to Zedekiah (2 Ki. 24:17).[79]

Hence, a 'name change' is a general feature of covenants that indicates one stands under a new authority and protection.

Conclusion

In addition to the essential elements of a covenant, which are present in all covenants of the first sense, additional features characterize a number of covenants. And although these features are catalogued under five headings, one readily recognizes some possible logical conclusions, each of which may also be supported by revelation. For example, if covenants are unilaterally dependent on the will of God, who also acts as its guarantor, it follows that the behavior of one or of both parties cannot break the covenant. It is dependent on God.[80]

Second, even though the behavior of the covenanters cannot destroy the agreement, compliance with the terms of the covenant are relevant, as discussed above. Compliance matters because each party in essence swore before God. Obligations are cosmic. They are not merely personal or social, but accountable to God, and therefore, moral. Consequently, failure to abide by covenant terms may threaten one's life.[81]

SUMMARY

In this chapter I began by exploring four major approaches that historically have been used to define the concept of covenant, noting strengths and weaknesses in each method: Julius Wellhausen's evolutionary approach; a philological approach; Walther Eichrodt's biblical-concept approach; and Gordon Hugenberger's biblical-concept approach. After demonstrating the superiority of Hugenberger's biblical-concept approach, which produced various "senses," I investigated the first sense of the term. Consequently, four essential elements of covenant were identified: (1) relationship; (2) with a non-relative; (3) involving obligations; and (4) is established under oath.

In addition to these covenant essentials, I also identified five general features. For instance, covenants are unilaterally dependent on the will and authority of God, resulting in morally binding obligations. Compliance with these terms, moreover, is relevant and tied to the reception of blessings and sanctions. I also showed that biblical covenants are often characterized by a sign that reflects the authority of the enacting party and itself expresses the covenant. Lastly, I noted that the name of the new dependent party in a covenant is changed to signal one stands under a new authority and protector. In chapter four I will seek to prove that God, at creation, designed marriage to be a covenant relationship by demonstrating the presence of the essential elements and general features of covenant in the paradigmatic relationship of Adam and Eve.

NOTES

1. See Walther Eichrodt, *Theology of the Old Testament*, trans. J. A. Baker (Philadelphia: Westminster, 1967); and Walter C. Kaiser Jr., *Toward an Old Testament Theology* (Grand Rapids: Zondervan, 1978). Several recent works survey the nature and meaning of "covenant" [tyriB.] in the Old Testament. See R. A. Oden, "The Place of Covenant in the Religion of Israel," in *Ancient Israelite Religion*, ed. P. D. Miller, P. D. Hanson and S. D. McBride (Philadelphia: Fortress, 1987); F. O. Garcia-Treto, "Covenant in Recent Old Testament Studies," *Austin Seminary Bulletin* 96 (1981); Walther Zimmerli, "The History of Israelite Religion," in *Tradition and Interpretation*, ed. G. W. Anderson (Oxford: Clarendon, 1979); Dennis J. McCarthy, *Old Testament Covenant: A Survey of Current Opinions* (Richmond, VA: John Knox, 1972); Delbert Roy Hillers, *Covenant: The History of a Biblical Idea*, Seminars in the History of Ideas (Baltimore, MD: Johns Hopkins, 1969); and R. Faley, "The Importance of the Covenant Conception in the Old Testament Religion," in *Rediscovery of Scripture: Biblical Theology Today* (Burlington, WI: Saint Francis College, 1967). For a discussion of these problem areas and scholars associated with them, see Gordon Paul Hugenberger, *Marriage As a Covenant: A Study of Biblical Law and Ethics Governing Marriage Developed From the Perspective of Malachi* (Leiden: Brill, 1994), 9.

2. In order to establish a definition for covenant, I will investigate the Old Testament word בְּרִית, since it is this word that would be most influential for Genesis. For an excellent discussion on the similarities and differences between בְּרִית., διαθήκη and συνθήκη, see Ellen Juhl Christiansen, *The Covenant in Judaism and Paul: A Study of Ritual Boundaries As Identity Markers* (Leiden: E.J. Brill, 1995), 8–11.

3. See Ernest W. Nicholson, *God and His People: Covenant and Theology in the Old Testament* (Oxford: Clarendon Press, 1986), 3–27. Nicholson begins his discussion of biblical covenants with the work of Julius Wellhausen, arguing that 'covenant' grew out of the preaching of the prophets. Against this view, Nicholson surveyed the works of Max Weber and Martin Noth. Nicholson describes the third phase of covenant research as the comparative study of Old Testament covenant and ancient Near Eastern treaties. Lastly, Nicholson writes that current studies are returning to Wellhausen's evolutionary position. Nicholson's own theory suggests the importance of covenant in ancient Israelite thought and not its reality in history or society.

4. Julius Wellhausen, *Prolegomena Zur Geschichte Israels* (Berlin: Walter de Gruyter and Company, 1927); This work was later published in English as Julius Wellhausen, *Prolegomena to the History of Israel* (New York: Meridian Books, 1957); and Julius Wellhausen, "Israel," in *Prolegomena to the History of Ancient Israel* (New York: Meridian Books, n.d.).

5. For other studies that explore the tradition-historical development of covenant in the Old Testament, see M. L. Newman, "The Continuing Quest for the Historical Covenant," in *The Psalms and Other Studies on the Old Testament*, ed. J. C. Knight and L. A. Sinclair (Nashotah, WI: Nashotah House Seminary, 1990); R. Davidson, "Covenant Ideology in Ancient Israel," in *The World of Ancient Israel*, ed. Robert E. Clements (Cambridge: Cambridge University Press, 1989); Hillers, *Covenant: The History of a Biblical Idea*; and Dennis J. McCarthy, *Treaty and Covenant: A Study in Form in the Ancient Oriental Documents and in the Old Testament* (Rome: Biblical Institute, 1981).

6. Ibid., 469. See also Nicholson, *God and His People: Covenant and Theology in the Old Testament*, 3–4.

7. Ibid., 5.

8. Wellhausen, *Prolegomena to the History of Israel*, 417–18.

9. Ibid.

10. McCarthy, *Old Testament Covenant*, 1–2.

11. See for example Moshe Weinfeld, "Berith," in *Theological Dictionary of the Old Testament*, ed. G. Johannes Botterweck, and Helmer Ringgren, trans. John T. Willis (Grand Rapids: William B. Eerdmans Publishing Company, 1975), 2:253–79. Also, for an excellent bibliography with regard to covenant studies, see Dennis J. McCarthy, *Old Testament Covenant: A Survey of Current Opinions* (Richmond, VA: John Knox Press, 1972), 90–198.

12. See J. Begrich, "*Berit*. Ein Beitrag zur Erfassung einer alttestamentlichen Denkform," *Zeitschrift für die alttestamentliche Wissenschaft* 60 (1944): 1–11. See also Gordon Paul Hugenberger, *Marriage As a Covenant: A Study of Biblical Law and Ethics Governing Marriage Developed From the Perspective of Malachi* (Leiden: E. J. Brill, 1994), 10.

13. McCarthy, *Old Testament Covenant*, 2.

14. See Ludwig Koehler, "Problems in the Study of the Language of the Old Testament," *Journal of Semitic Studies* 1 (1956): 4–7. See also Ed Meyer, *Die Israeliten Und Ihre Nachbarstamme* (Halle: Max Niemeyer, 1906); J. Barton Payne, "Covenant," in *The Zondervan Pictorial Encyclopedia of the Bible*, ed. Merrill Tenney (Grand Rapids: Zondervan, 1976), 1:1002; H. C. Leupold, *Exposition of Genesis* (Grand Rapids: Baker, 1942), 2:488; W. F. Albright, "The Hebrew Expression for 'Making a Covenant' in Pre-Israelite Documents," *BASOR* 121 (February 1951): 22; and Hugenberger, *Marriage as a Covenant*, 170.

15. See McCarthy, *Old Testament Covenant*, 3; F. Charles Fensham, "Did a Treaty Between the Israelites and the Kenites Exist?" *BASOR* 175 (October 1964): 54; and Weinfeld, "Berith," 253–54.

16. Ibid., 255.

17. Ibid., 255.

18. Ibid.

19. See A. Jepsen, "*berith*. Ein Beitrag zur Theologie der Exilzeit," *Rudolph Fetschrift*, Tubingen, 1961, 161–80.

20. Walther Eichrodt, *Theology of the Old Testament*, trans. J.A. Baker (Philadelphia: Westminster Press, 1967).

21. See ibid., 30. See also Rolf Rendtorff, "Approaches to Old Testament Theology," in *Problems in Biblical Theology: Essays in Honor of Rolf Knierim*, ed. Henry T. C. Sun and Keith L. Eades (Grand Rapids: William B. Eerdmans Publishing Company, 1997), 13–7.

22. Eichrodt, *Old Testament Theology*, 11.

23. See Hayes and Prussner, *Old Testament Theology: Its History and Development*, 181.

24. Eichrodt, *Old Testament Theology*, 13–4.

25. See Hayes and Prussner, *Old Testament Theology: Its History and Development*, 183.

26. See James Barr, *The Semantics of Biblical Language* (London: Oxford University Press, 1961), 238.

27. For a discussion of a "concept oriented" approach for understanding the "sense" of words, see Cotterell and Turner, *Linguistics and Biblical Interpretation*, 146–54. Cotterell and Turner equate a concept oriented method with the traditional approach. "Roughly speaking, the descriptive sense of a word is taken to be the bundle of meaning we might otherwise call the concept denoted by the word. Accordingly, if we want to know the sense of the word 'cup', we sit down and puzzle out a definition of 'cup' that encompasses its characteristic and distinctive features. This is then regarded as the sense of the word cup."

28. This phenomenon of a single lexeme having multiple senses is called polysemy. See ibid., 136.

29. Ibid., 151.

30. See Hugenberger, *Marriage as a Covenant*, 168–215.

31. Ibid., 171.

32. G. E. Mendenhall, "Covenant," ed. Buttrick, George Arthur, The Interpreter's Dictionary of the Bible: An Illustrated Encyclopedia (Nashville: Abingdon Press, 1962), 2:714. See also Meredith G. Kline, who defined covenant as, "A sanction-sealed commitment to maintain a particular relationship or follow a stipulated course of action. In general, then a covenant may be defined as a relationship under sanctions, " in Meredith G. Kline, *By Oath Consigned: A Reinterpretation of the Covenant Signs of Circumcision and Baptism* (Grand Rapids: William B. Eerdmans Publishing Company, 1968), 16

33. See Hugenberger, *Marriage as a Covenant*, 172.

34. McCarthy, *Old Testament Covenant*, 10. George Mendenhall was the first to explore this relationship in his *Law and Covenant in Israel and the Ancient Near East* (Pittsburgh: The Biblical Colloquium, 1955). For a survey of works in this area, see McCarthy, *Old Testament Covenant*, 10–34. Also, see Philip J. Calderone, *Dynastic Oracle and Suzerainty Treaty: 2 Samuel 7: 8–16* (Manila: Ateneo University Publications, 1966), 9–14.

35. See James Barr, *The Semantics of Biblical Language* (London: Oxford University Press, 1961), 238.

36. Hugenberger, *Marriage as a Covenant*, 175.

37. Not all scholars accept the centrality of "relationship" to tyriB.. For example, see Nicholson, *God and His People: Covenant and Theology in the Old Testament.*

38. Hugenberger, *Marriage as* Covenant, 176–77.

39. See Hugenberger, *Marriage as a Covenant*, 177. See also M. Weinfeld, "*Berith*" in *Theological Dictionary of the Old Testament*, ed. G. Johannes Botterweck, trans. John T. Willis (Grand Rapids: William B. Eerdmans Publishing Company, 1975), 2:225–79; Joseph A. Fitzmyer, "The Matthean Divorce Texts and Some New Palestinian Evidence," *Theological Studies* 37 (1976): 204; William A. Heth and Gordon J. Wenham, *Jesus and Divorce: The Problem with the Evangelical Consensus* (Nashville: Thomas Nelson Publishers, 1994), 103; and Paul Hoffman, "Jesus' Saying About Divorce and Its Interpretation in the New Testament Tradition," *Concillium* 55 (1970): 55–6.

40. See Dennis J. McCarthy, *Treaty and Covenant: A Study in Form in the Ancient Oriental Documents and in the Old Testament* (Rome: Biblical Institute, 1981), 106. In addition, McCarthy discussed familial analogies and covenants, though he understands marriage at times to be a contract rather than a covenant: McCarthy, *Old Testament Covenant*, 33–4.

41. Paul Kalluveettil, *Declaration and Covenant: A Comprehensive Review of Covenant Formulae From the Old Testament and the Ancient Near East* (Rome: Biblical Institute Press, 1982), 212.

42. William A. Heth, "Jesus on Divorce: How My Mind Has Changed," *Southern Baptist Journal of Theology* vol. 6, no. 1 (Spring 2002): 18.

43. McCarthy, *Old Testament Covenant*, 33.

44. See discussion in Hugenberger, *Marriage as a Covenant*, 178. If Hugenberger's analysis is correct and covenants do in fact extend relationships beyond the natural unity, this understanding would support the thesis that marriage is a covenant. Stated differently, if marriage is a covenant, then it too would extend relationships beyond natural ties; and thus, according to Leviticus 18 and 20, one is equally forbidden to have sexual relations with an affine or consanguine.

45. See E. Kutsch, *Verheissung und Gesetz. Untersuchungen zum sogennanten ‚Bund' im Alen Testament*, BZAW 131 (Berlin: Walter de Gruyter, 1973) 28–39.

46. Weinfeld, "*Berith,*" 2:255.

47. McCarthy, *Old Testament Covenant*, 3.

48. Ibid. See also Weinfeld, "*Berith,*" 2:256; and Gene M. Tucker, "Covenant Forms and Contract Forms," *Vetus Testamentum* 15 (1965): 500.

49. Weinfeld, "*Berith,*" 2:256.

50. For a list of texts that associate "covenant" with "oath," see Hugenberger, *Marriage as a Covenant*, 184. For a contrast between covenants and contracts, see Tucker, "Covenant Forms and Contract Forms," 500. Tucker states covenants are based on the oath pattern and contracts are not.

51. See Exod. 32:1–6.

52. Waltke, "The Phenomenon of Conditionality within Unconditional Covenants," 135. Additionally, Waltke writes, "God's grant of seasonal harvest and blessing are in space and time universally irrevocable, but locally and temporarily conditional upon moral behavior or providential acts. Both the irrevocable and conditional aspects of the covenant further man's spiritual life." Ibid., 127.

53. Cotterell and Turner, *Linguistics and Biblical Interpretation*, 151.

54. Hugenberger, *Marriage as a Covenant*, 175.

55. Ralph Elliott, *The Message of Genesis* (Nashville: Broadman Press, 1961), 170.

56. Hugenberger, *Marriage as a Covenant*, 184.

57. See ibid., 177. See also M. Weinfeld, "*Berith*" in *Theological Dictionary of the Old Testament*, ed. G. Johannes Botterweck, trans. John T. Willis (Grand Rapids: William B. Eerdmans Publishing Company, 1975), 2:225–79; Joseph A. Fitzmyer, "The Matthean Divorce Texts and Some New Palestinian Evidence," *Theological Studies* 37 (1976): 204; William A. Heth and Gordon J. Wenham, *Jesus and Divorce: The Problem with the Evangelical Consensus* (Nashville: Thomas Nelson Publishers, 1994), 103; and Paul Hoffman, "Jesus' Saying About Divorce and Its Interpretation in the New Testament Tradition," *Concillium* 55 (1970): 55–6.

58. See also Prov. 2:16–18 and Ezek. 16:9–14, 60–63 which not only demonstrate the relevance of covenant compliance but also extend the idea to the marriage relationship.

59. George Wesley Buchanan, *The Consequences of the Covenant* (Leiden: Brille, 1970), 131. See also Ezek. 33:16.

60. See also Exo 31:17 and Jos 4:6. For a discussion of the differences between signs and symbols, see Millard J. Erickson, *Christian Theology* (Grand Rapids: Baker Book House, 1983), 1093–1097.

61. See Gen. 9:15, 16; Exod. 6; Lev. 26:42, 45; Deut. 8:18; 33:9; 2 Ki. 13:23; 1 Chr. 16:15; Neh. 13:29; Ps. 89:29; Ps. 103:18; Ps. 106:45; Jer. 3:16; Jer. 14:21; Jer. 31:34; Ezek. 16:60, 61, 63; Amos 1:9; Lk. 1:72; Heb. 8:12; 10:17.

62. See Deut. 4:23, 31; 8:19; 2 Ki. 17:38; Ps. 74:19.

63. See Gen. 31; Deut. 7:9; Neh. 9:8; Ps. 78:37; Isa. 49:7; Hos. 11:12.

64. See Gen. 6:18; 17:9, 10, 11; Exod. 19:5; Lev. 26:9; Deut. 7:9; 12; Josh. 3:3; Jos. 7:11; 1 Ki. 8:23; 1 Ki. 11:11; 2 Ki. 17:38; 23:2, 3; 2 Chr. 6:14; 23:3; 34:30, 31, 32; Ps. 25:10; Ps. 78:10; Ps. 103:18; Ps. 132:12; Isa. 42:6; 49:8; 56:4, 6; Jer. 11:8; 2 Cor. 3:14; Heb. 9:20.

65. See Exod. 31:17; Jos. 4:7; 1 Chr. 16:15; 2 Chr. 13:5; 2 Chr. 21:7; Ps. 55:19; 74:19; 79:13; 89:2, 4, 28, 29; 105:8; 111:5, 9; Isa. 59:21; Ezek. 37:25, 26; Hos. 2:19; Heb. 7:21.

66. Elmer B. Smick, "*Karat*," in *Theological Wordbook of the Old Testament*, ed. R. Laird Harris, Gleason L. Archer and Bruce K. Waltke (Chicago: Moody Press, 1980), 457. See also discussion in Meredith G. Kline, *By Oath Consigned: A Reinterpretation of the Covenant Signs of Circumcision and Baptism* (Grand Rapids: William B. Eerdmans Publishing Company,

1968), 16. Kline also links the idea of "cutting a covenant" with circumcision, which also was a sign of the covenant.

67. When Jesus instituted the Lord's Supper, he stated that the wine signified "my blood of the covenant" (Matt 26:27). Perhaps Christians are encouraged to "count the cost" of entering a covenant relationship with Christ because of the relationship's permanent nature (Luke 14:28).

68. The following discussion comes from a currently unpublished paper by David Jones and myself, which I presented at the Southeast Regional meeting of the Evangelical Theological Society, Louisville, Kentucky, March 19, 2005: "Are Biblical Covenants Dissolvable?: Toward a Theology of Marriage."

69. Köstenberger, *God, Marriage, and Family*, 239, 246.

70. Heth, "Jesus on Divorce," 17.

71. Hugenberger, *Marriage as a Covenant*, 3.

72. Köstenberger notes these same fourteen examples in his footnote reference to Hugenberger, *Marriage and Family*, 409, n. 54.

73. Num. 30:12–13 (in English versions).

74. James Barr, *The Semantics of Biblical Language* (London: Oxford University Press, 1961), 238. See also D.A. Carson, *Exegetical Fallacies* (Grand Rapids: Baker Books, 1996), 60–61.

75. See, for example, Gen. 21:27; Exod. 2:24; Lev. 26:42; 2 Ki. 13:23; 1 Chr. 16:16; Ps. 105:9; Acts 3:25; and Acts 7:8.

76. Ralph Alexander, *Ezekiel* in The Expositor's Bible Commentary, vol. 6 (Grand Rapids: Zondervan, 1986), 818.

77. Francis Ian Andersen and David Noel Freedman, *Hosea* in Anchor Bible Commentary, vol. 24 (New York: Doubleday, 1980), 221.

78. One who places himself under the authority of Jesus Christ accordingly takes the name of Christ and consequently is called *Christ*ian. See also 2 Sm 12:28.

79. Henri Blocher, *In the Beginning: The Openning Chapters of Genesis* (Leicester, England and Downers Grove: InterVarsity Press, 1984), 91. Also, see Hugenberger, *Marriage as Covenant*, 164.

80. For a comparison of covenants and contracts, see Paul F. Palmer, "Christian Marriage: Contract or Covenant?" *Theological Studies* 33 (December 1972): 619–20. Palmer contends covenants can be breached but not broken, thus indicating the lasting nature of covenants.

81. It is not by accident that entrance into a covenant relationship was often accompanied by blood from a sacrificed animal. See Matt 26:27; Zech 9:11; and Ps 50:5.

Chapter 4

Marriage as Covenant in Genesis 1 and 2

Chapter one outlined three ways the church historically understood and discussed the institution of marriage: as a covenant, as a sacrament, and as a contract. In outlining these three approaches, a new question emerged: Are these three approaches equally valid systems for viewing marriage, with each one merely emphasizing different facets of the marriage relationship? Or, is one accurate to the exclusion of the other two? God designed marriage to be a covenant relationship; however, the present crisis surrounding the institution of marriage arises, in large measure, from people viewing marriage as a contract rather than a covenant.

What evidence supports the thesis that God designed marriage to be a covenant relationship, and why is it important? In this chapter I address both the importance and the difficulty of recognizing the covenant nature of marriage from the beginning. I then present arguments from Genesis and Malachi supporting the claim that God designed marriage to be a covenant relationship from the beginning.

IMPORTANCE AND DIFFICULTY OF IDENTIFYING THE COVENANTAL NATURE OF MARRIAGE FROM THE BEGINNING

Why is it important to establish that God, in the beginning, designed marriage as a covenant relationship? Did God originally create marriage as a covenant relationship or did man create the idea of covenant marriage? If God made marriage a covenant at creation, then the covenant nature is *essential* to the basic meaning of marriage.

Karl Barth addresses the importance of creation ordinances in *Ethics*. Referring to God's creation ordinances, Barth claims all Christians stand under these commands:

> When we speak of *existing* orders, we mean orders that do not exist accidentally, that exist in certain historical relations, that stand or fall in these relations. . . .There are . . . *orders of creation*, i.e., orders that come directly into question (and more than that) with the fact of our life itself as representatives of *the* order, as a creaturely standard and basis of knowledge of the will of the Creator, as words which we cannot possibly overlook in obedience to *the* Word because they are set on our lips and in our hearts with our life as direct testimonies to *the* Word, as words that could not be any different in any historical situation: primal words to which all historically developed and fashioned orders, and all serious attempts to change or overthrow them, must always refer back and appeal as at their penultimate basis, primal words which at all events proclaim God's own Word, which cannot be questioned as representatives of God's order, which always *are* representatives of that order, which in all circumstances describe the uniform and necessary binding which makes our conduct good and which cannot, therefore, be *not* respected in obedience to God's command.[1]

Thus, Barth claims God, in the beginning, consciously designed certain orders as a basis for knowing and understanding his will. Indeed, these orders are universal and necessarily binding. Old Testament scholar Walter Kaiser similarly contends that creation ordinances manifest the work of God in creation and "depict 'the constitution of things' as they were intended to be from the Creator's hand. They cover and regulate the whole gamut of life."[2] Hence, if marriage was established as a covenant from the beginning, it is both essential and binding on all men in all cultures for all times.

Since בְּרִית, the Hebrew term for 'covenant,' does not occur in the first two chapters of Genesis, some assume the idea of covenant marriage must also be absent. How can one defend the covenantal nature of marriage in Genesis, much less in the husband-wife relationship of Adam and Eve, when the term 'covenant' is not employed in the first two chapters of Genesis?

Opponents of Trinitarian theology have used similar arguments to defend the unity of the Godhead. David Bernard, pastor of New Life United Pentecostal Church in Austin, maintains that terms such as *Father* and *Holy Spirit* are only titles for God:

> Trinitarians sometimes explain that the Old Testament monotheistic passages merely speak of perfect agreement and unity among the trinity, excluding a plurality of false deities but not a plurality of persons in the true God. This view would allow outright polytheism, however, for many distinct deities could exist in perfect harmony. Moreover, neither the Old Testament writers nor their original

> audiences thought of God as trinity. . . . Neither testament uses the word *trinity* or associates the word *three* or the word *persons* with God in any significant way. No passage says God is a holy two, holy three, or holy trinity, but over fifty verses call God the "Holy One" (Isaiah 54:5).[3]

M. S. KcKinney, pastor of Friendship Apostolic Church, uses a similar argument in his book *60 Questions on the Godhead with Bible Answers*: "Is the word *Trinity* in the Bible? No. Does the Bible say that there are three persons in the Godhead? No."[4] Thus, based on the absence of the word *trinity*, the United Pentecostal Church concludes the doctrine of the trinity must be heretical.[5]

Despite the absence of *trinity* from Scripture, however, orthodox Christians historically have believed that God is a trinity. On this, for example, Alister McGrath in his *Christian Theology* expresses the majority, orthodox view saying:

> The Foundations of the doctrine of the Trinity are to be found in the pervasive pattern of divine activity to which the New Testament bears witness. The Father is revealed in Christ through the Spirit. There is the closest of connections between the Father, Son, and Spirit in the New Testament writings. Time after time, New Testament passages link together these three elements as part of a greater whole. The totality of God's saving presence and power can only, it would seem, be expressed by involving all three elements. The same Trinitarian structure can be seen in the Old Testament.[6]

Thus, McGrath contends that a pattern pervades the Scriptures without which it would be impossible to express "the totality of God's saving presence and power." The history of Christianity demonstrates biblical truth does not ultimately rise or fall on the presence of a word, but rather, on the cumulative weight of evidence in Scripture.

Historically, Christians have defended the validity of various theological concepts even though, like the doctrine of the Trinity, a key term for the doctrine is absent from the Bible. Of special interest to this study, Eugene Merrill has argued the presence of a covenant in the early chapters of Genesis, despite the absence of the term 'covenant' in the first three chapters:

> Because Genesis is the book of beginnings it is not surprising that covenant should first be found there, and, in fact, found in more specific instances than anywhere else in the Bible. So fundamental is the covenant theme there it is not an exaggeration to say that Genesis provides the principal statement of God's purposes of which the remainder of the biblical witness is an enlargement and interpretation.[7]

Thus, Merrill claims the presence of covenant in the first three chapters of Genesis, even though the term 'covenant' does not appear in the text.[8]

Like Merrill, other scholars endorse theological concepts even in the absence of a key term. Paul Kalluveettil records:

> The word 'covenant' poses a problem. Although the most frequent term for covenant is *berit* (287 occurrences) there are in the OT numerous references to covenants and covenant relationships where the term does not occur. It is illogical to restrict the study only to those texts where the word *berit* occurs. Covenant seems to be a broad category which includes *berit* passages as well as other texts which contain the ideas even though not always verbally expressed.[9]

In his *Theology of the Old Testament*, Walther Eichrodt likewise notes:

> The crucial point is not—as an all too naïve criticism sometimes seems to think—the occurrence or absence of the Hebrew word *berit* . . . The actual term 'covenant' is, therefore, so to speak, only the codeword for a much more far-reaching certainty, which formed the very deepest layer of the foundations of Israel's faith, and without which indeed Israel would not have been Israel at all.[10]

Although proving the presence of covenant in Genesis 1 and 2 would be easier if the term appeared, lack of the precise term does not necessarily preclude the presence of covenant. To the contrary, the precise word is nothing more than a linguistic reference to the reality itself.[11] The reality can be present without the linguistic reference, even if the linguistic reference would make the reality much easier to prove.

ARGUMENTS SUPPORTING THE COVENANTAL NATURE OF MARRIAGE FROM THE BEGINNING

Although it is difficult to demonstrate in the opening chapters of Genesis that God designed marriage to be a covenant relationship, the church should not eschew this challenge because of the importance for understanding marriage as God intended. I am convinced that Scripture provides at least three clues to God designed marriage as a covenant relationship: (1) by the presence of the essential elements of a covenant in Genesis; (2) by the presence of some general features of a covenant in Genesis; and (3) by textual arguments in Malachi.

Essential Elements Argument from Genesis 1 and 2

Demonstrating the presence of covenant in Genesis 1 and 2, as noted earlier, does not rest necessarily on the presence of the term. Since the term בְּרִית does not appear in the first two chapters of Genesis, what evidence supports the thesis that God, at creation, designed marriage to be a covenant relationship? Building on the four essential elements of covenant outlined in chapter two, I will demonstrate the presence of each in the paradigmatic relationship of Adam and Eve.

In chapter two, I used a biblical-concept approach to define covenant. Consequently, I identified four essential elements present in all biblical covenants of the first sense: (1) personal relationship; (2) with a non-relative; (3) involving obligations; and (4) established under oath.

Personal Relationship

Of the four essential covenant elements, 'personal relationship' is the easiest to demonstrate in the first two chapters of Genesis.[12] Except for creation itself, the predominant theme in chapters one and two is relationship, whether between God and man, man and beast, or between husband and wife. The author of Genesis prepares the reader for the husband-wife relationship with several literary clues. In the creation account of humanity, for example, the author introduces subtle differences distinguishing the creation of man from God's earlier creative acts. First, rather than the customary jussive, "Let there be," verse twenty-six begins with the first person cohortative, "Let us make."[13] Second, Genesis records the creation of man by announcement rather than command.[14] Third, rather than being created "according to its own kind," as previous creatures were, humanity is created according to the likeness of God. Fourth, only humans were given the charge of dominion over "fish of the sea, over the birds of the air, and over every living thing that moves on the earth." Last, Scripture specifically refers to the creation of humankind as "male and female." To this point in the narrative, the author has not considered gender a detail worth stressing. Hence, being made male and female is significant.[15]

In this creation account, God not only creates humanity in his image, but he creates them differently. Although man and woman both equally bear the image of God, a sexual duality exists.[16] Moreover, whatever God does, he does for a reason. In his treatise, *The Estate of*

Marriage (1522), Luther comments on Genesis 1:27: "From this passage we may be assured that God divided mankind into two classes, namely, male and female, or a he and a she." [17] By introducing the creation of man as male and female, therefore, the author of Genesis prepares the reader for relationship, namely the relationship between a husband and wife.

Karl Barth insists the author of Genesis supplied another literary clue of relationship when he wrote, "Let us make man in our image, according to our likeness; So God created man in his own image; in the image of God he created him; male and female he created them" (Gen 1:26–27). Barth contends "Let us" refers to a counterpart in God's being. That is, a relationship exists in the Godhead, "a free co-existence and co-operation; an open confrontation and reciprocity."[18] In the same manner, Barth views humanity as the "repetition" of this divine form:

> Thus the *tertium comparationis*, the analogy between God and man is simply the existence of the I and the Thou in confrontation. This is first constitutive for God, and then for man created by God. To remove it is tantamount to removing the divine from God as well as the human from man. [19]

Barth believed humans exist in a relationship with God analogous to the relation that exists within the Godhead. Barth summarized his position, "In this way, [God] wills and creates man as a partner who is capable of entering into covenant-relationship with Himself."[20] God made mankind male and female with the possibility of confrontation similar to the relationship existing within the Godhead.

In chapter one, the author notes the creation of humanity in God's image is closely related to being made male and female. In chapter two, God develops more clearly at what he hinted earlier, and he creates woman, demonstrating creation in the image of God involves a relationship between man and his wife. The author of Genesis introduces another literary clue of relationship in verse eighteen, recording the words of God, "And it is not good" (Gen 2:18). The Lord's evaluation of man's solitude is "not good." However, this appraisal in no way contradicts his previous decree of "good." To the contrary, the latter expression merely connotes man's incompleteness. Accordingly, God reveals his intentions to create for man a "helper comparable to him [עֵזֶר כְּנֶגְדּוֹ]."[21] By creating a helper, God suggests the husband's strength is inadequate by itself (compare Isa 30:5; Ezk 12: 14; and Hos 13:9). [22] And so, Delitzsch concludes, "Human beings cannot fulfill their destiny in any other way than in mutual assistance."[23] God made man for a relationship.

In verses twenty-three and twenty-four, the author supplies two more indications of 'relationship' in Genesis. First, the author of Genesis uses a "relational formula" to record Adam's response to the creation of Eve.[24] Second, in verse twenty-four he writes, "Therefore a man shall leave his father and mother and be joined to his wife." No doubt the author has in mind the husband-wife relationship. By introducing the creation of humanity with subtle differences from earlier creative acts by God, the author prepares the reader for something significant—the creation of man as male and female. Then the author focuses his discussion from the broad male-female relationship to the specific husband-wife relationship by recording God's creation of a helper and the relational formula. Clearly, the essential element 'relationship' is present in the Genesis narrative.

With A Non-relative

The second essential element of biblical covenants is 'non-relative.'[25] That is, covenants are elected relationships that extend family boundaries beyond present familial attachments. The author of Genesis implies biblical marriage involves the establishment of a new family unit between unrelated persons when he records a man must "leave" and "cleave" and the two become "one flesh." Nevertheless, some commentators dispute this interpretation of verse twenty-four.

Some critics, for example, maintain the idea of leaving and cleaving preserves aspects of a matriarchal society, contending the wife exercised authority over the husband in the absence of his father and mothers.[26] Within the same narrative, however, Scripture records, "And he shall rule over you" (Gen 3:16), affirming the husband's authority over his wife. Thus, the idea of matriarchy fails on exegetical grounds.[27]

To leave and be joined to one's wife stresses the basic need for the husband to reorient completely his total allegiance and devotion for his parents to his wife. A necessarily literal interpretation of leave is unwarranted, "as if this term could refer only to a change in domicile."[28] Rather, 'leave' should be seen more figuratively.[29] The Old Testament as a whole expresses this view.

For example, when Abraham sent his chief servant to obtain a wife for his son Isaac, the servant prayed for God to reveal to him the woman whom he should choose. After the Lord answered his prayer by showing him Rebekah, he responded, "Blessed *be* the LORD God of my master Abraham, who has not forsaken [לֹא־עָזַב] His mercy and His truth toward my master. As for me, being on the way, the LORD led me to the house of my master's brethren" (Gen 24:27). In this passage, the servant did not literally intend that the LORD God had not "left" Abraham, but rather, God had not abandoned his loyalty to his servant Abraham.[30]

To leave, therefore, while it may include a literal move from one house to another, does not necessitate it, but rather, figuratively refers to the establishment of a new family unit and loyalty to it. As a result, one assumes new responsibilities and obligations. Accordingly, Cassuto writes, "To leave and cleave simply means that when a man takes a wife, he creates a new family. So long as he is in his father's house, all his love is dedicated to his father and mother, but when he marries, his love for his wife transcends that for his parents."[31] Leaving denotes the establishment of a new family unit, and cleaving points to the committed faithfulness that one promises to the other; "that whatever the future holds, the couple intend to face it as a pair."[32]

The Pentateuchal author also intends a new family unit when he writes, "And they shall become one flesh." While some scholars have submitted that "to become one flesh" is an allusion to offspring or to be equated with sexual union, their contentions cannot be sustained under closer scrutiny.[33] Clearly, sexual union is involved, evidenced by the following verse, "They were both naked, the man and his wife, and were not ashamed" (Gen 2:25). Subsequent Scripture, however, negates equating "one flesh union" with sexual intercourse. Instead, the one flesh union appears to be the result of sexual intimacy. New Testament records, "Or do you not know that he who is joined to a harlot is one body *with her?* For 'the two,' He says, 'shall become one flesh'" (1 Cor 6:16). Likewise, Matthew writes, "For this reason a man shall leave his father and mother and be joined to his wife, and the two shall become one flesh. So then, they are no longer two but one flesh. Therefore what God has joined together, let not man separate" (Matt 19:5–6; see also Mark 10:6–9). Hence, they *become* one flesh as a result of sexual union. One flesh refers to a new and continuing nature. "In other words, it is doubtful that the reader is to imagine that following the consummation of the marriage in sexual union or following each successive act of intercourse, the couple reverts to their former state of being two separate fleshes!"[34] And so one flesh union succinctly expresses the establishment of a new family unit.

Involving Obligations

The third essential element of biblical covenants is ‘obligation,’ what McCarthy calls the covenant’s conditions.[35] All covenants have obligations.[36] Four arguments help demonstrate the presence of ‘obligation’ in the first two chapters of Genesis, providing additional evidence that God designed marriage to be a covenant relationship from the beginning. First, immediately after creating humanity as male and female in his image, God tasks him with several responsibilities, such as being fruitful, filling and subduing the earth, and having dominion over every living thing on the earth. Being made in the image of God involves fulfilling certain obligations. Mankind acts as God’s representative rulers on earth, serving under his dominion.[37]

Second, to assist man with his obligations, God created a helper, which connotes functional responsibility.[38] That is, a helper assists, supports, and facilitates another. Something is required of both the helper and the one being helped. By creating a helper, God implies the man’s strength is inadequate by itself.[39] God meant for humanity to live in a relationship of mutual assistance, implying the presence of ‘obligation.’[40]

A third argument supporting the presence of ‘obligation’ in Genesis stems from the command to leave and cleave. Whereas leaving points to the establishment of a new family unit, cleaving indicates one’s faithfulness to another.[41] By cleaving, couples promise never to leave or forsake the other, “till death do us part.”

Fourth, the idea of ‘one flesh’ also indicates the presence of obligations. Biblical writers often use ‘one flesh’ [בְ’שַׂר]” synonymously with ‘one clan’ or ‘one kindred group.’[42] In Leviticus, for example, the author writes, “His uncle or his uncle’s son may redeem him; or *anyone* who is near of kin [בְ’שָׂרוֹ] to him in his family may redeem him” (Lev 25:49; see also Gen 29:14; Lev 18:6; and 2 Sm 5:1). The author demonstrates one flesh not only identifies one’s family, but it also implies obligations to the individuals identified. In Leviticus, the obligation is to redeem another. Therefore, four examples of the essential element ‘obligation’ support the claim covenant is present in the first two chapters of Genesis.

Established under Oath

The fourth essential element of a biblical covenant is ‘oath.’ Thus far it has been demonstrated that Genesis speaks of marriage using covenant concepts. What remains is whether or not this relationship is established by an oath. The author of Genesis implies biblical marriage involves an oath by using the "relational formula," providing additional evidence that marriage is a covenant relationship.[43]

The phrases "bone of my bones and flesh of my flesh" signifies a relationship. It is a figure of speech signifying kinship.[44] For example, when Abimelech returned to his mother's house in Shechem, he attempted to persuade the people to follow him by reminding them of his kinship stating, "Remember that I am your own flesh and blood (Judg 9:2)." Similarly, as all the tribes of Israel came to David at Hebron, they pleaded for him to be their king asserting, "We are your own flesh and blood" (2 Sm 5:1; also see 2 Sm 19:12 and 1 Chron 11:1). And so, while agreeing with von Rad that Adam is seeking to express a supreme joy, the verse appears to suggest further that Eve is a member of his family—his wife.[45]

Second, Brueggemann contends that the "relationship formula" is "a covenant oath which affirms and establishes a pattern of solidarity."[46] The relationship formula implies more than a familial relationship; it includes loyalty and reciprocal allegiance.[47] The second person singular, "*You* are now bone of my bones" is conspicuously absent. Rather, Adam expresses himself to God, "*This* is bone of my bones." And so, "These words appear to have been intended as a solemn affirmation of his marital commitment, an elliptical way of saying something like, 'I hereby invite you, God, to hold me accountable to treat this woman as part of my own body.'"[48] Therefore, the relationship of Adam and Eve contains the essential elements of a covenant, providing evidence that God designed marriage to be a covenant relationship from the beginning. That is, Adam and Eve represent a relationship of unrelated individuals established by an oath before God with obligations. Having demonstrated the presence of the essential elements of a covenant in the first two chapters of Genesis, I now turn to demonstrating that several general features characterizing biblical covenants are also present in the marriage of Adam and Eve.

General Features Argument from Genesis 1 and 2

As previously stated, demonstrating the presence of covenant in Genesis 1 and 2 does not rest necessarily on the presence of the term בְּרִית. As the covenant nature of the first marriage in the first two chapters of Genesis was illustrated by observing the presence of essential elements of covenant in the relationship God established between Adam and Eve, one may also establish the presence of covenant by recognizing the presence of general features associated with biblical covenant discussed earlier in chapter two.

Unilaterally Dependent on the Will and Authority of God

The first general feature of a biblical covenant identified in chapter two was covenants are unilaterally dependent on the will and authority of God. One may also recognize the presence of this feature is present in the marriage of Adam and Eve. As a third party member to all covenants, Calvin wrote, God guarantees the relationship.[49] Calvin reasoned that man is incapable of abolishing what God establishes. "Unless the Lord builds the house, they labor in vain who build it" (Ps 127:1). Consequently, if marriage is established by God as a covenant relationship, it unilaterally depends on his will and authority.

Scripture consistently affirms that God established covenant marriage. "For by Him all things were created that are in heaven and that are on earth, visible and invisible, whether thrones or dominions or principalities or powers. All things were created through him and for him" (Col 1:16). More importantly, however, God established marriage in the first chapters of Genesis. The author of Genesis depicts a loving God who, upon recognizing that it was not good for man to be alone, fashioned Eve and brought her to Adam, effectively creating the first marriage (Gen 2:22). Subsequent Scripture affirms this conclusion. Malachi writes, "Did not the Lord make them one" (Mal 2:15; see also Matt 19:6)? Consequently, God assures the marriage relationship. Because God created covenant marriage, man possesses neither the power nor authority to destroy it.[50]

A Covenant Sign

The second general feature of a biblical covenant identified in chapter two was that covenants are recognized and sealed by a sign. This feature is also present in the paradigmatic relationship of Adam and Eve where the two are joined in one flesh union. Although it is not explicitly stated, sexual intercourse most likely represents the covenant sign of Adam and Eve's marriage.[51] Biblical writers, including the author of Genesis, consistently identify sexual intercourse as the decisive act for consummating the marriage relationship.[52] Consider, for example, how Israel assimilated women captured in war into their society:

> When you go out to war against your enemies, and the LORD your God delivers them into your hand, and you take them captive, and you see among the captives a beautiful woman, and desire her and would take her for your wife, then you shall bring her home to your house, and she shall shave her head and trim her nails. She shall put off the clothes of her captivity, remain in your house, and mourn her father and her mother a full month; after that you may go in to her and be her husband, and she shall be your wife [וְהָי'תָה לְךָ לְא'שָּׁה וְאַחַר כֵּן 'תָּבוֹא אֵלֶי'הָ וּבְעַל'תָּהּ]. And it shall be, if you have no delight in her, then you shall set her free, but you certainly shall not sell her for money; you shall not treat her brutally, because you have humbled her (Deut 21:10–14).[53]

By having sexual intercourse ['תָּבוֹא אֵלֶי'הָ] with the woman, the two became husband and wife. Accordingly, Hugenberger writes the Deuteronomist does not record three distinct events in time: the husband "goes into her" ['תָּבוֹא אֵלֶי'הָ], "he becomes her husband" [וּבְעַל'תָּהּ], and later "she becomes his wife" [וְהָי'תָה לְךָ לְא'שָּׁה]. "Rather, the last two clauses are epexegetical and, as such, are simultaneous reciprocal consequences of the first clause."[54]

The story of Jacob and Leah provides a second example of sexual intercourse validating and sealing a marriage. After completing seven years of labor for Laban in exchange for his daughter Rachel, Jacob requested: "Give me my wife, for my days are fulfilled that I may go in to her [וְ'אָבוֹ'אָה אֵלֶי'הָ]" (Gen 29:21). Here, Jacob is not merely informing Laban that he intends to have sexual relations [וְ'אָבוֹ'אָה אֵלֶי'הָ] with his daughter, but rather, he means to consummate the marriage. That is, sexual intercourse is understood as the sign of covenant marriage; it validates and seals the relationship. Even though Laban deceived Jacob into having sexual intercourse with Leah, Jacob never challenged the validity of his 'marriage' with Leah. The consequences of his actions were permanent.[55] Hence, Scripture often depicts sexual relations as the sign of covenant marriage.

Not only does Scripture indicate that sexual intercourse is the sign of covenant marriage, but more importantly, the sign is present in the marriage of Adam and Eve. The author of Genesis records that the husband is to leave his father and mother and be joined to his wife, "and they shall become one flesh." While some scholars have submitted that "to become one flesh" is an allusion to offspring or to be equated with sexual union, their contentions cannot be sustained under closer scrutiny.[56] Nevertheless, sexual union clearly is involved, evidenced by the following verse, "They were both naked, the man and his wife, and were not ashamed" (Gen 2:25). Consistent with this interpretation, the author later records "Now Adam knew [יָדַע"] Eve his wife, and she conceived" (Gen 4:1).[57] By Scripture consistently identifying sexual intercourse with the sign of marriage, and by the author of Genesis making explicit reference to the one flesh union, being naked, and Adam "knowing" his wife, sufficient evidence exists for recognizing the presence of the general feature 'sign of the covenant' in the marriage of Adam and Eve.

A Name Change

The last general feature present in the marriage relationship of Adam and Eve is a name change. After God presented Eve to Adam, Adam acknowledges his covenant responsibility to provide and protect her by naming her: "This *is* now bone of my bones and flesh of my flesh; She shall be called Woman [אִשָּׁה], because she was taken out of Man" (Gen 2:23). By renaming Eve, Adam confirmed she was under his authority, thus placing on himself certain covenant responsibilities.

Scripture is replete with similar examples of a name change within a covenant relationship. For instance, God changed Jacob's name to Israel and Abram's name to Abraham upon entering a covenant relationship with each. More significantly, however, Christians take the name of Christ upon entering a covenant relationship with him (Acts 11:26).[58] As a result of entering into a covenant relationship with Christ, which is reflected by taking his name, Christians stand under the authority and protection of Christ, who is the stronger partner within the covenant. Likewise, by assuming the husband's name, a wife signifies to others that a marriage covenant has been established and that she now stands under the protection and authority of her husband.

Therefore, the relationship of Adam and Eve contains general features of a covenant, providing evidence that God designed marriage to be a covenant relationship from the beginning. Not only does the presence of the essential elements and general features of biblical covenants in the first two chapters of Genesis provide credible clues that God established a covenant marriage between Adam and Eve, but textual evidence in Malachi provides serious hints of this truth as well.

Textual Arguments from Malachi 2:10–16

Possibly the clearest way to prove that God, at creation, designed marriage as a covenant relationship comes from direct textual evidence in Malachi 2. Speaking the inspired words of God, Malachi not only claims marriage was a covenant at the time he wrote, but also that it was established by God as a covenant at creation:

> Because the LORD has been witness between you and the wife of your youth, with whom you have dealt treacherously; Yet she is your companion and your wife by covenant. But did He not make them one, having a remnant of the Spirit? And why one? He seeks godly offspring. Therefore take heed to your spirit, and let none deal treacherously with the wife of his youth (Mal 2:14–16).

After Malachi accuses the men of Israel of dealing treacherously with their wives and profaning the marriage covenant, he appeals to Genesis 2:24, the text that defines marriage as God designed it. By appealing to the paradigmatic relationship of Adam and Eve as the reason to respect marriage as a covenant, Malachi effectively declares that God made marriage a covenant when he established it in the beginning. Some commentators, however, challenge this interpretation of Malachi, unconvinced of the following two contentions: that "covenant" in Malachi 2:14 refers to a literal marriage and that Malachi 2:15 is an appeal to Genesis 2:24. The following two exegetical arguments answer these challenges.

Arguments that Support Identifying 'Covenant' in Verse 14 as a Literal Marriage

Flemming Hvidberg rejects identifying the "covenant" in verse fourteen with a literal marriage, writing instead that it refers to the relationship between God and Israel: "'the wife of thy youth' . . . and 'the wife of thy covenant' . . . are similies which denote the cult of Yahweh, the faith in Yahweh. Yahweh is himself very nearly 'the wife of youth', with whom Judah had a covenant."[59] Because verses ten and fourteen appear within the same pericope, one may expect the term covenant to have the same reference. Moreover, the two verses have parallel structures, such as their common charge of unfaithfulness against Israel and the allusions to the creation narrative.

Although these observations permit a common identification of covenant in verses fourteen and ten, they do not require it. Second, no marriage analogies in Scripture portray God as the wife. To the contrary, in marriage analogies between Israel and Judah and God, Scripture always depicts Israel and Judah as the wife. Third, it is doubtful that God would be a "witness," as the first half of verse fourteen asserts, *and* the "wife," as the second half of verse fourteen suggests. Last, Malachi does not use the term 'covenant' in a univocal manner. Malachi references the covenant between Yahweh and Israel and the covenant of Levi within a span of six verses (Mal 2:4, 5, 8, 10). Consequently, "there can be no inherent objection to the view that Malachi intends yet another reference by his use of covenant in 2:14."[60] Therefore, insufficient evidence exists for identifying the covenant in verse fourteen with the relationship between God and Israel instead of identifying it as a literal marriage.

Second, by equating the expression "the daughter of a foreign god" in verse eleven with a goddess and not a literal bride, some commentators reason the entire passage must be figurative; thus, they reject identifying 'covenant' in verse fourteen with a literal marriage.[61] Two arguments, however, mitigate against identifying the phrase "daughter of a foreign god" with goddess. First, it is doubtful that Malachi would choose the ambiguous phrase "daughter of a foreign god" rather than using the clear term 'goddess' or even naming the goddess. Second, because Malachi is writing to fellow Israelites, who are children of Yahweh, then "by definition a pagan woman would be the daughter not of Yahweh, but of a 'foreign god.'"[62] Malachi's reasoning follows from his rhetorical question in verse ten: "Have we not one father?" Because the phrase "daughter of a foreign god" merely represents another means of recognizing a pagan woman, insufficient evidence exists for identifying 'covenant' in verse fourteen figuratively rather than identifying it as a literal marriage.

Third, some commentators reject identifying 'covenant' in verse fourteen as a literal marriage based upon the larger context of the book of Malachi. For example, G. W. Ahlström contends, "Malachi is always interested primarily in what he himself considers to be a pure and right Yahweh cult, and the social and moral problems are not his main concern here."[63] In other words, Ahlström suggests because Malachi's primary concern is with cultic matter rather than personal and social ethics, Malachi 2:14 must not be about marriage. However, recognizing that Malachi emphasizes cultic offenses is quite different from saying cultic offenses are Malachi's exclusive concern.[64] Malachi records Yahweh's warning "against sorcerers, against adulterers, against perjurers, against those who exploit wage earners and widows and orphans, and against those who turn away an alien" (Mal 3:5). One is hard pressed to reduce each of these threats to mere cultic transgressions. Although Malachi stresses cultic matters, this does not necessitate the avoidance of personal and social ethics. Therefore, no credible arguments exist for overturning the traditional identification of 'covenant' in verse fourteen as a literal marriage. In addition to answering the above objections, two supplementary positive lines of reasoning also support the traditional identification of 'covenant' as a literal marriage.

First, the parallel structure in verse fourteen between "the wife of your youth" and "the wife of your covenant" implies that the covenant was between a husband and a wife. Thus, the covenant in verse fourteen communicates a literal marriage between a man and a woman, consistent with the traditional interpretation.[65]

Second, not only is the phrase "the wife of your covenant" parallel with "the wife of your youth," it is in apposition to the expression "your companion." When Malachi states the Lord was a witness between the men of Israel and their companions, he clarifies what he means with the phrase, "the wife of your covenant," implying marriage is a covenant relationship with God as its witness. Therefore, the term 'covenant' in verse fourteen refers to a literal marriage between a man and a woman, and objections to this identification based upon structure, the interpretation of "the daughter of a foreign god," and the overall message of the book are all inadequate.

Arguments that Support Interpreting Malachi 2:15 as an Appeal to Genesis 2:24

Four reasons support interpreting Malachi 2:15 as a direct appeal to Genesis 2:24, the text that defines marriage as God designed it. The first argument that supports interpreting Malachi 2:15 as an appeal to Genesis 2:24 is that Malachi appears closely associated with the Pentateuch. R. L. Smith writes:

> The language and ideas of Malachi are deeply influenced by the Deuteronomic materials. "Love," "fear," "faithlessness" are motifs occurring frequently in Deuteronomy and in Deuteronomic history.... The "law of Moses" "Horeb," "all Israel" in Mal 3:22 (Eng. 4:4) is Deuteronomic.[66]

Throughout the book, Malachi applies Deuteronomic emphases to the circumstances of his day.[67] Based upon their common motifs, vocabulary, and emphases, therefore, Malachi demonstrates strong reliance on the Pentateuch. As a result, one is not surprised to find allusions to Genesis.

A second argument that supports interpreting Malachi 2:15 as an appeal to Genesis 2:24 is verse fifteen's close association with verse ten, which appeals to Genesis. Verses ten and fifteen use common terminology and concepts, such as the terms 'one' [אחד] and 'treacherously' [בגד]. Both verses also employ creational imagery by means of the verbs בראנו and עשה, although it is clear that Malachi does not intend the first creation, but the calling of a people unto himself.[68] Lastly, the expression "one Father to us all" [אב אחד לכלנו] in verse ten prepares one to identify the phrase "Godly seed" [זרע אלהים] in verse fifteen with the Genesis narrative, strengthening the tie between verses ten and fifteen and supporting the claim that Malachi appeals to Genesis 2:24 in verse fifteen.

A third argument that supports interpreting Malachi 2:15 as an appeal to Genesis 2:24 is that both Genesis and Malachi underscore the responsibility of the husband toward his wife. Upon Adam's recognition of Eve as "bone of my bones and flesh of my flesh," Genesis records Adam's obligation to "leave" and to "cleave." Similarly, Malachi contends a husband is obliged to be faithful to his wife. Dealing "treacherously" with one's wife constitutes possible harm to one's life: "Take heed of your life [ונשמרתם ברוחכם]." By implication, Malachi and Genesis instruct the husband to act responsibly toward his wife, supporting the claim that Malachi appeals to Genesis 2:24 in verse fifteen.

A fourth argument that supports interpreting Malachi 2:15 as an appeal to Genesis 2:24 is that Malachi uses the term אחד intentionally to link verse fifteen to the Genesis narrative and particularly to the paradigmatic relationship of Adam and Eve. Malachi asks, "And did he (Yahweh) not make them one (אחד)?"[69] By making reference to the one flesh union of Adam and Eve, Malachi insists that the married couples of his own day must, like the first couple, concede God made them "one." Besides this expression, no stronger connection between Malachi and Genesis exists. Therefore, based upon Malachi's strong relationship with the Pentateuch, his common terms and concepts with Genesis, and especially his emphasis that God makes couples one in marriage, sufficient evidence exists for claiming that Malachi appeals to the first marriage in verse fifteen. Malachi underscores the claim that God, at creation, designed marriage to be a covenant relationship by emphasizing the nature of marriage as a covenant in verse fourteen and appealing to Genesis as the basis for that claim.

SUMMARY

I began this chapter began by showing the importance of whether or not God designed marriage to be a covenant relationship from the beginning, positing that if God made marriage a covenant at creation, then covenant is *essential* to the basic meaning of marriage. Second, I argued the absence of the term ברית from the first chapters of Genesis does not indicate necessarily 'covenant' is not present. It is illogical to restrict the study of 'covenant' only to those texts where the word occurs.[70] The precise word is nothing more than a linguistic reference to the reality itself. The reality can be present without the reference.

Next, I presented arguments from Genesis and Malachi that support the claim that God, at creation, designed marriage to be a covenant relationship. The essential elements and general features arguments in Genesis and the logical and textual arguments in Malachi provide substantial evidence that God designed marriage to be a covenant relationship at creation. In the next chapter I will seek to demonstrate that subsequent Scripture dealing with marriage not only does not contradict the idea of its covenant nature but supports it as well.

NOTES

1. Karl Barth, *Ethics*, ed. Dietrich Braun, trans. Geoffrey W. Bromiley (Zuerich: Theologischer Verlag, 1928–1929; reprint, Edinburgh: T. & T. Clark, 1981), 215.
2. Walter C. Kaiser Jr., *Toward Old Testament Ethics* (Grand Rapids: Zondervan Publishing Company, 1983), 31. For a discussion of the "orders of creation," see Carl F. H. Henry, *Christian Personal Ethics* (Grand Rapids: William B. Eerdmans Publishing Company, 1957), 242–6; John Murray, *Principles of Conduct: Aspects of Biblical Ethics*, 2d ed. (Grand Rapids: William B. Eerdmans Publishing Company, 1994), 27–81.
3. Doctrines of the Bible, 17–18.
4. M. S. McKinney, www.bromac.com/Godhead/Godhead.htm.
5. For and excellent bibliography of works about the Apostolic Church or United Pentecostal Church International, see *A Guide to the Study of the Pentecostal Movement* by Charles Edwin Jones (Metuchen, New Jersey: The Scarecrow Press), 1983.
6. Alister E. McGrath, *An Introduction to Christian Theology* (Oxford University: Blackwell Publishers, 1997), 293.
7. Eugene Merrill, "Covenant and the Kingdom: Genesis 1–3 As Foundation for Biblical Theology," *Criswell Theological Review* 1, no. 2 (1987): 297–8.
8. בְּרִית appears, though in various forms, twenty-seven times in Genesis, or about one-tenth of all uses in the Old Testament. See ibid., 298.
9. Paul Kalluveettil, *Declaration and Covenant: A Comprehensive Review of Covenant Formulae From the Old Testament and the Ancient Near East* (Rome: Biblical Institute Press, 1982), 3.
10. Walther Eichrodt, *Theology of the Old Testament*, trans. J.A. Baker (Philadelphia: Westminster Press, 1967), 17–8.
11. For further discussion see Gordon Paul Hugenberger, *Marriage As a Covenant: A Study of Biblical Law and Ethics Governing Marriage Developed From the Perspective of Malachi* (Leiden: E. J. Brill, 1994), 157. Also see G.

E. Mendenhall, "Covenant," ed. Buttrick, George Arthur, The Interpreter's Dictionary of the Bible: An Illustrated Encyclopedia (Nashville: Abingdon Press, 1962), 2:715: "There are numerous references to covenants and covenant relationships where this term does not occur."

12. Although the essential element 'personal relationship' is broad, seemingly including contracts or promises as well, it is unique to covenant. Covenants are solemn agreements between nations, peoples, or individuals, such as marriage. Contracts, on the other hand, are used of property or of personal belongings. "When persons are involved, it is not the person who is hired or contracted for, but his services. A man is hired to do something." See Paul F. Palmer, "Christian Marriage: Contract or Covenant?" *Theological Studies* 33 (December 1972): 619.

13. History has supplied various attempts to explain the plural forms: "Let us make man in our image, according to our likeness." For an excellent summary of these interpretations, see Claus Westermann, *Genesis 1–11: A Commentary*, trans. John J. Scullion (Minneapolis: Augsburg Publishing House, 1984), 144–45. Westermann discusses possible solutions under four headings: (1) reference to the Trinity; (2) reference to God and a heavenly court; (3) an attempt to avoid any immediate resemblance of humans to God; and (4) a plural of deliberation.

14. See Ralph Elliott, *The Message of Genesis* (Nashville: Broadman Press, 1961), 36.

15. John H. Sailhamer, *The Pentateuch As Narrative* (Grand Rapids: Zondervan Publishing Company, 1992), 94–5.

16. No major commentators dispute that the image of God is equally shared by both sexes, although some authors, such as Gilbert Bilezikian, argue as if a major debate exists. See Raymond C. Ortlund, "Male-Female Equality and Male Headship: Genesis 1–3," in *Recovering Biblical Manhood & Womanhood: A Response to Evangelical Feminism*, ed. John Piper and Wayne Grudem (Wheaton, Illinois: Crossway Books, 1991), 97–8.

17. Martin Luther, "The Estate of Marriage (1522)" in *Luther's Works*, ed. Walther I. Brandt and Helmut T. Lehmann, trans. Walther I. Brandt (Philadelphia: Muhlenberg Press, 1962), 45:17.

18. Ibid., 3.1.185.

19. Ibid.

20. Ibid.

21. For a helpful discussion of this expression, see Dorothy Jean Kelley Patterson, "Aspects of a Biblical Theology of Womanhood" (Ph. D. diss., University of South Africa, 1997), 119–30.

22. See Gordon J. Wenham, *Word Biblical Commentary*, ed. David A. Hubbard et al., vol. 1, *Genesis 1–15* (Waco, TX: Word Books, 1987), 68.

23. C. F. Keil and F. Delitzsch, *Biblical Commentary on The Old Testament*, trans. James Martin, vol. 1, *The Pentateuch* (Grand Rapids: William B. Eerdmans Publishing Company, 1971).

24. For a discussion regarding the "relationship formula,"see N. P. Bratsiotis, "*Basar*," ed. Botterweck, G. Johanness, Ringgren, Helmer, trans. John T.

Willis, Theological Dictionary of the Old Testament (Grand Rapids: William B. Eerdmans Publishing Company, 1975), 2:319. The idea of "relational formula" will be discussed later under the element 'oath.'

25. Clearly, a contract, a friendship, or even a treaty could establish a relationship with a non-relative as well. The presence of a single essential element does not establish a covenant. Because the elements are essential, all four must be present. In fact, a treaty may be a covenant, but not all covenants are treaties. See Hugenberger, *Marriage as Covenant*, 172.

26. See Gerhard von Rad, *Genesis: A Commentary*, The Old Testament Library, trans. John H. Marks (Philadelphia: Westminster Press, 1972), 85.

27. U. Cassuto, *A Commentary on The Book of Genesis*, trans. Israel Abrahams, vol. 1, *From Adam to Noah: Genesis 1–6* (Jerusalem: Magnes Press, 1961), 137. For additional critique on the idea of matriarchy, see also Mace, *Hebrew Marriage: A Sociological Study*, 35–94.

28. Hugenberger, *Marriage As a Covenant*, 159.

29. In Genesis 2:24, "leave" translates the Hebrew עָזַב.

30. For other passages that reflect this use of "leave," see: Deut 28:20; 29:25; 31:8, 16, 17; and Josh 1:5.

31. Cassuto, *From Adam to Noah*, 137.

32. David J. Atkinson, *The Message of Genesis 1–11*, The Bible Speaks Today, no. 1, ed. J. A. Motyer and John R. W. Stott (Downers Grove, IL: InterVarsity Press, 1990), 75.

33. See Von Rad, *Genesis*, 85; and John Skinner, *The International Critical Commentary: A Critical and Exegetical Commentary*, ed. Samuel Rolles, Alfred Plummer and Charles Augustus, vol. 1, *Genesis* (New York: Charles Scribner's Sons, 1910), 70; For detailed refutation of these views, see Hugenberger, *Marriage as a Covenant*, 160–2.

34. See Atkinson, *The Message of Genesis 1–11*, 76, who agrees that one flesh "does not only mean sexual intercourse, though it includes it. But it refers to that oneness which—initially in intention, and gradually more and more a reality through time—marks a good marriage relationship. Sexual intercourse is thus given a meaning: it is meant to express, consolidate and deepen the 'one flesh' union of man and wife, as they grow more and more together in a relationship which expresses something of God. More than that, 'one flesh' may also point to the link between sexuality and creativity which brings marriage and family life together." Morris writes concerning one flesh: "[One flesh] refers to the sexual act, which unites husband and wife in the most intimate fashion." Leon Morris, *The Gospel According to Matthew* (Grand Rapids: William B. Eerdmans Publishing Company, 1992), 481.

35. See Dennis J. McCarthy, *Old Testament Covenant: A Survey of Current Opinions* (Richmond, VA: John Knox Press, 1972), 3.

36. In chapter six, I will identify various theological truths stemming from marriage being covenant relationship. Accordingly, we will elaborate on the precise nature of covenant obligations. For example, they are moral, cosmic, and unconditional.

37. See also Hans Walter Wolff, *Anthropology of the Old Testament* (Philadelphia: Fortress Press, 1973), 160; and G. C. Berkouwer, *Man: The Image of God*, trans. Dirk W. Jellema (1957; reprint, Grand Rapids: William B. Eerdmans Publishing, 1962). See also Dale Moody, *The Word of Truth: Summary of Christian Doctrine Based on Biblical Revelation* (Grand Rapids: William B. Eerdmans Publishing, 1990), 226; and Paul Ramsey, *Basic Christian Ethics* (1950; reprint, Louisville: Westminster, 1993), 250–64. I am not suggesting, as Moody advocates, a functional view of the image of God. That is, although the image of God involves something one does, it also involves substantive elements. For a more complete presentation of the functional view, see Anthony Hoekema, *Created in God's Image* (Grand Rapids: William B. Eerdmans Publishing Company, 1986), 33–65.

38. Although function does not presuppose obligation, functional *responsibility* does. A husband is morally obligated to provide spiritual leadership for his family. This is one of his functional responsibilities. This is quite different from saying because one spiritually leads his family, he is obligated to do so. Because the woman was created *for* helping, she is obligated necessarily to do so. Failure on her part is sin.

39. See Wenham, *Genesis*, 68.

40. On this point, Stanley Grenz appears to confuse function, such as helping, with an outcome, such as being saved. 'Helper' connotes a function that may or may not be accepted, much less fulfilled. This mistake engenders Grenz to forsake a functional difference God intends in verse eighteen. See Stanley J. Grenz, *Sexual Ethics: An Evangelical Perspective*, 2d ed. (Dallas: Word Publishing Company, 1990; reprint, Louisville, KY: Westminster John Knox Press, 1997), 32.

41. Atkinson, *The Message of Genesis* 1–11, 75.

42. See Skinner, *Genesis*, 70.

43. See Bratsiotis, "*Basar*," 2:319.

44. See Bruce Vawter, *On Genesis: A New Reading* (Garden City, NY: Doubleday and Company, 1977), 75; and Cassuto, *From Adam to Noah*, 135.

45. See Von Rad, Genesis, 84; and Hugenberger, *Marriage as a Covenant*, 164–5.

46. Walter Brueggemann, "Of the Same Flesh and Bone," *Catholic Biblical Quarterly* 32 (1970): 535.

47. Hugenberger, *Marriage as a Covenant*, 230–1.

48. Ibid., 231.

49. John Calvin, trans. John Owen, vol. 5, *Commentaries on the Twelve Minor Prophets: Zechariah and Malachi* (Grand Rapids: William B. Eerdmans Publishing Company, 1950), 552–3. For a discussion on God's presence and role in covenants, see also See also M. Weinfeld, "*Berith*" in *Theological Dictionary of the Old Testament*, ed. G. Johannes Botterweck, trans. John T. Willis (Grand Rapids: William B. Eerdmans Publishing Company, 1975), 2:225–79; Joseph A. Fitzmyer, "The Matthean Divorce Texts and Some New Palestinian Evidence," *Theological Studies* 37 (1976): 204; William A. Heth and Gordon J. Wenham, *Jesus and Divorce: The Problem with the Evangelical*

Consensus (Nashville: Thomas Nelson Publishers, 1994), 103; and Paul Hoffman, "Jesus' Saying About Divorce and Its Interpretation in the New Testament Tradition," *Concillium* 55 (1970): 55–6.

50. See discussion of marriage as a covenant in Witte, *From Sacrament to Contract*, 95. Also, see Calvin's sermon on Ephesians 5:22–26: "Marriage is not a thing ordained by men. We know that God is the author of it, and that it is solemnized in his name. The Scripture says that it is a holy covenant, and therefore calls it divine." Also, in his sermon on Deuteronomy 5:18: Marriage is called a covenant with God . . . meaning that God presides over marriages."

51. For a discussion of the differences between signs and symbols, see Millard J. Erickson, *Christian Theology* (Grand Rapids: Baker Book House, 1983), 1093–1097. Recall that a sign is both a validating seal and an expression of the covenant relationship itself.

52. For a discussion concerning sexual intercourse as the decisive act for consummating a marriage, see Abel Isaksson, *Marriage and Ministry in the New Temple: A Study with Special Reference to Mt. 19:13-12 (Sic) and 1. Cor. 11:13–16* (Copenhagen: C. W. K. Gleerup Lund, 1965), 23

53. In chapter six, I will argue for the indissolubility of the marriage relationship. Consequently, I interpret the phrase "then you shall set her free" to refer to a non-sexually consummated relationship.

54. Hugenberger, *Marriage as Covenant*, 249.

55. For additional examples of sexual intercourse consummating the marriage relationship, see Deut 25.5; Gen 38:8, 18; Exod 22:15; and Deut 22:28. Also, for a discussion of the legal consequences of premarital and extramarital sex, see Hugenberger, *Marriage as Covenant*, 251–267.

56. See Von Rad, *Genesis*, 85; and John Skinner, *The International Critical Commentary: A Critical and Exegetical Commentary*, ed. Samuel Rolles, Alfred Plummer and Charles Augustus, vol. 1, *Genesis* (New York: Charles Scribner's Sons, 1910), 70; For detailed refutation of these views, see Hugenberger, *Marriage as a Covenant*, 160–2.

57. For a discussion concerning the association of the term יָדַע" and its sexual use in conjunction with covenant passages, see Herbert B. Huffmon and S. B. Parker, "A Further Note on the Treaty Background of Hebrew יָדַע"," *Bulletin of the American Schools of Oriental Research* 181 (1996): 31–38. Huffmon and Parker contend the term יָדַע" means "to recognize the authority of," which stems from its use in treaties. That is, each party of the treaty "recognizes" the other as covenant partners. See also Hugenberger, *Marriage as Covenant*, 268–69.

58. Interestingly, Christians make up the church—the bride of Christ. The covenant relationship between Christ and the church is recognized as a marriage.

59. Flemming Friis Hvidberg, *Weeping and Laughter in the Old Testament: A Study in Canaanite-Israelite Religion* (Leiden: E. J. Brill, 1962), 123.

60. Hugenberger, *Marriage as Covenant*, 27–8.

61. Hvidberg, *Weeping and Laughter*, 121–23.

62. Hugenberger, *Marriage as Covenant*, 34–5.

63. Gösta Werner Ahlström, *Joel and the Temple Cult of Jerusalem*, Supplements to *Vetus Testamentum* (Leiden: E. J. Brille, 1971), 51.

64. Hugenberger, *Marriage as Covenant*, 41.

65. Ibid., 28.

66. Smith, *Micah-Malachi*, 300.

67. R. J. Coggins, *Haggai, Zechariah, Malachi*, Old Testament Guides (Sheffield: JSOT Press, 1987), 76. See also Smith, *The Book of the Twelve Prophets*, 327–30

68. See Hugenberger, *Marriage as a Covenant*, 148–49.

69. Not all commentators agree on the antecedent of the pronoun 'he' in verse fifteen. See Smith, *A Critical Commentary of Malachi*, 54-55: "This is a possible translation of [the Masoretic Text], though there is no indication that the first clause is interrogative. . . . To whom does the pronoun "he" refer? . . . Some make God the subject and treat "one" as equivalent to "one flesh" . . . Others make "one" the subject and identify it with Abraham . . . Still others have made it more general in scope, viz. 'No one has done it.'" Three reasons support understanding Yahweh to be the subject of the first phrase וְלֹא-א'הד ' ע'שׂה. First, this interpretation allows one to accept the Masoretic Text as it stands, without emending it. Second, inverted word order in the expression וְלֹא-א'הד ' ע'שׂה supports identifying the phrase as an interrogative clause. Third, interpreting the initial expression as a question with Yahweh as the subject receives substantial support from other scholars, which demonstrates this interpretation falls well within the mainstream of credible research. For example, see W. Emery Barnes, *Malachi: With Notes and Introduction*, The Cambridge Bible for Schools and Colleges, ed. A. F. Kirkpatrick (Cambridge: Cambridge University Press, 1917), 13–4; Ebenezer Henderson, *The Book of the Twelve Minor Prophets: Translated From the Original Hebrew with a Commentary, Critical, Philological, Exegetical* (London: Hamilton, Adams, and Company, 1858), 454–5; T. T. Perowne, *Malachi: With Introduction and Notes*, The Cambridge Bible for Schools and Colleges, ed. A. F. Kirkpatrick (Cambridge: Cambridge University Press, 1910), 26–7; Smith, *Micah-Malachi*, 319; John Edgar McFadyen, "Malachi," in *The Abingdon Bible Commentary*, ed. Frederick Carl Eiselen, Edwin Lewis and David G. Downey (Nashville: Abingdon Press, 1929), 835; John Calvin, trans. John Owen, vol. 5, *Commentaries on the Twelve Minor Prophets: Zechariah and Malachi* (Grand Rapids: William B. Eerdmans Publishing Company, 1950), 554–6; Dummelow, *A Commentary on the Holy Bible*, 614; A. R. Faussett, "Malachi," in *The Definitive Bible Commentary*, ed. Owen Collins (London: Harper Collins Publishers, 1999), 874; E. B. Pusey, *The Minor Prophets with a Commentary: Explanatory and Practical, and Introductions to the Several Books* (London: James Nisbet and Company, 1907), 229; and Clarke, *Concise Bible Commentary*, 627.

70. Kalluveettil, *Declaration and Covenant*, 3.

Chapter 5

Marriage as Covenant Elsewhere in Scripture

In the previous chapter I presented arguments from Genesis and Malachi demonstrating God, at creation, designed marriage to be a covenant relationship. By proving that all of the essential elements and general features of a biblical covenant were present in the relationship of Adam and Eve and that Malachi not only refers to marriage as a covenant but appeals to Genesis for the basis of that claim, I provided substantial evidence that God designed marriage to be a covenant relationship at creation. In this chapter I will seek to demonstrate that subsequent passages in Scripture dealing with marriage are consistent with this interpretation.

HOSEA 2:18–22

If God designed marriage from the beginning to be a covenant relationship, subsequent passages dealing with marriage should not contradict this interpretation. In fact, an examination of these passages provides further evidence of the covenantal nature of marriage. In particular, those passages describing Yahweh's relationship to Israel in terms of a marriage offer key evidence for understanding marriage as a covenant. Hosea, for example, views marriage as a covenant based upon a parallel of Yahweh's relationship with Israel. Yahweh explicitly refers to his relationship with Israel as a covenant when he describes Israel's unfaithfulness: "But like men they transgressed the covenant; there they dealt treacherously with me" (Hos 6:7; see also Hos 8:1). Hosea similarly identifies marriage as covenant in two ways.

First, the covenant between God and Israel parallels the marriage between Hosea and his wife. Using the prophetic names of Hosea's children, God threatens to dissolve his covenant with Israel stating, "You are not my people, and I will not be your God" (Hos 1:9). Hosea, likewise, threatens to dissolve his marriage asserting, "For she is not my wife and I am not her husband" (Hos 2:2). But while both God and Hosea claim to sever their corresponding relationships, both threats of dissolution are followed with unanticipated promises of restoration. Yahweh exclaims, "Yet the number of the children of Israel shall be as the sand of the sea, which cannot be measured or numbered. And it shall come to pass in the place where it was said to them, 'You *are* not my people,' *There* it shall be said to them, '*You are* sons of the living God'" (Hos 1:10). Hosea accordingly retracts his earlier threat declaring his promise of a new marriage (Hos 2:14–23).[1] This structural parallelism underscores the identification of marriage as covenant in Hosea.[2]

A second basis for recognizing marriage as a covenant in Hosea is the presence of divorce and covenant-forming formulae.[3] Hosea's statements, "She is not my wife, and I am not her husband" (Hos 2:1) and Yahweh's claim, "You are my people, and I will be your God" (Hos 2:23) are similar to formulae used elsewhere in the ancient Near East for entering covenants. Considerable evidence also supports the identification of Hosea 2:1 as a divorce formula.[4] Jeremiah, a book many authors claim is heavily influenced by Hosea, records Yahweh gave Israel a certificate of divorce (Jer 3:8).[5] Based upon the book's parallel structure and covenant-forming phrases, therefore, Hosea equates the relationships between God and Israel and Hosea and his wife, thus identifying marriage as a covenant.

PROVERBS 2:16–17

Whereas marriage is viewed as a covenant by analogy in Hosea, it is stated explicitly in Proverbs. According to Proverbs, wisdom produces moral discernment and deliverance from evil—the adulteress woman: "To deliver you from the immoral [ז’רָה”] woman, from the seductress [מ”נכְר”יָה] *who* flatters with her words, who forsakes the companion of her youth, and forgets the covenant of her God" (Prov 2:16–17). Although the majority of commentators equate "covenant of her God" with marriage, thus identifying marriage as a covenant, two additional interpretations of this phrase have also been posited.[6]

First, some researchers maintain the expression "covenant of her God" refers to a pagan deity because the Hebrew adjectives מ”נכְר”יָה and ז’רָה” describing "woman" may be translated "foreign" and "strange."[7] Hence, given that the woman was a "stranger" and "foreigner," her actions betray the covenant she has with *her* god. Furthermore, since Proverbs 1–9 consistently uses Yahweh to refer to God, Bostrom contends that אלהים most likely refers to a pagan deity.[8]

Five arguments mitigate against this interpretation. First, אלהים appears in synonymous parallel with יהוה in Proverbs 2:5 and thus undeniably refers to the God of Israel. Similarly, אלהים surfaces in Proverbs 3:4 where it also clearly refers to the true God. Therefore, its appearance in 2:17 as a reference to the God of Israel is not without correspondence within Proverbs 1–9. Second, the phrase "covenant of her God" requires attaching the pronominal suffix "her" to "God" [אלהי’ה]. Since the pronominal suffix in Hebrew is never attached to יהוה the author had no choice but to use אלהים and therefore, no particular significance should be attached to this option. Third, it is doubtful the author of Proverbs condemns this woman for an offence against her pagan deity, but rather he emphasizes the wrong committed against the true God. Fourth, although covenants between pagan deities and their followers appear in Scripture, it happens so rarely that it is doubtful it would appear in the book of Proverbs. Lastly, Bostrom and others fail to successfully argue for translating מ”נכר”יה and ז’רה” "foreign" and "strange."[9] McKane, for example, holds the woman described in verse sixteen is merely estranged from the corporate life of her community.[10] Toy nicely concludes:

> The general character of the descriptions here . . . makes it almost certain that the writer has in mind dissolute women without regard to nationality, and that the *strange woman* is one who is not bound to the man by legal ties, who is outside the circle of his proper relations, that is, a harlot or an adulteress.[11]

Therefore, sufficient evidence does not exist for interpreting "covenant of her God" as a pagan deity.

Second, some researchers maintain the expression "covenant of her God" refers to the Sinaitic Covenant. For example, Murphy states, "As it stands, [the covenant of her God] does not preclude further refinement, e.g., the symbolism of the covenant between the Lord and Israel."[12] Kidner agrees that verse seventeen refers to the covenant at Sinai, but interestingly observes had the author intended the marriage covenant, the wording of verse seventeen would have followed Malachi 2:14.[13] Thus, Kidner accedes marriage is a covenant, but merely doubts its appearance in Proverbs 2:16–17.

Claudia Camp's work on the parallels between Proverbs 2 and Malachi 2 presents a convincing argument against interpreting "the covenant of her God" as a reference to Sinai.[14] The phrase "forsakes the companion of her youth" in Proverbs 2:17 resembles "to be faithless to the wife of his youth" in Malachi 2:16. Also, "companion" in Proverbs 2:17 equates with "companion" in Malachi 2:14. Lastly, "forgets the covenant of her God" in Proverbs 2:17 corresponds to "against whom you have been faithless, though she is . . . your wife by covenant" in Malachi 2:14. Therefore, if Malachi refers to the marriage covenant, which was shown earlier, then Proverbs' association with it lends credence to perceiving the covenant in verse seventeen as the marriage covenant. Therefore, the phrase "covenant of her God" in Proverbs should be equated with marriage since alternative interpretations fail under exegetical scrutiny.

EZEKIEL 16:8

Ezekiel 16:8 represents another Old Testament passage deserving examination regarding the nature of covenant marriage: "When I passed by you again and looked upon you, indeed your time *was* the time of love; so I spread my wing over you and covered your nakedness. Yes, I swore an oath to you and entered into a covenant with you, and you became mine." Within this passage, commentators often debate three major exegetical difficulties. First, scholars are less than univocal regarding the identity of Jerusalem. Greenberg, for example, considers Jerusalem a figure of speech for the people of God.[15] Alternatively, Eichrodt and others identify Jerusalem with the Davidic Dynasty and inhabitants of the city.[16] Fortunately, the historical identification of Jerusalem is not crucial to recognizing the covenant nature of marriage from this passage.

The second exegetical complexity in this verse concerns the intended meaning of the phrase, "I spread my skirt over you, and covered your nakedness." Three reasons support identifying the phrase with a literal covering rather than sexual intercourse.[17] First, symbolic actions associated with Near Eastern marriages were often accompanied with literal garments, lending credence to their plausible use in Israelite marriages. Second, since the expression "to uncover the nakedness of" someone is commonly understood as a figure of speech for sexual intimacy, it is unlikely "to cover the nakedness of," which is found in Ezekiel 16:8, would also refer to sexual union. Lastly, Hugenberger avers, "If the 'covering' mentioned in Ezek. 16:8 refers to sexual union, the resulting order of sexual union preceding betrothal would be anomalous and, as such, would be unexpected as a description of divine activity."[18] Hence, covering another's nakedness most likely does not connote sexual intercourse, but rather, a literal act typically performed during the marriage ceremony.

Allen describes the Lord's actions as a marriage rite with accompanying responsibilities: "For a man to spread the hem of his garment over a woman was a symbolic gesture that constituted a proposal of marriage. He thus extended over her both his authority and his willingness to support her."[19] Wevers agrees with Allen claiming the phrase "to cover the nakedness" symbolizes the husband's protection of his wife.[20] While it is unclear exactly what obligations attended the covering, such as ownership, provision, and protection, the expression used in Ezekiel 16:8 appears to represent a covenant oath with accompanying responsibilities, supporting the claim of marriage as a covenant.

The third area of controversy in verse eight regards the identification of the covenant. Some scholars understand the covenant mentioned in verse eight as the covenant God entered with Israel at Sinai. Calvin, for example writes, "There is no doubt that this ought to be referred to the promulgation of the law. . . . God deservedly announces 'that he had come into covenant' because he then coupled the people to himself."[21] Calvin agrees Ezekiel uses the language and metaphor of marriage. However, he does not view the covenant expressed in 16:8 as the marriage covenant. Rather, Calvin views it as the Sinaitic Covenant, where God joined himself to the people of Israel.

Alternatively, the majority of interpreters identify the "covenant" as marriage for two reasons. First, Ezekiel 16 appears to be closely related to Malachi 2 and Proverbs 2, both of which were shown earlier to speak of marriage as a covenant relationship. Second, because Ezekiel maintains the marriage metaphor throughout the entire chapter, it is doubtful that he would have suddenly abandoned his theme in order to discuss the covenant at Sinai.[22] Therefore, Ezekiel 16:8 bolsters the claim that God designed marriage as a covenant relationship.

In this section I surveyed Old Testament passages that support the claim marriage has always been a covenant institution. Whereas Malachi appeals directly to the creation narrative in Genesis, other passages, such as Hosea 2, Proverbs 2, and Ezekiel 16, reinforced the idea, metaphorically describing the covenant relationship between God and Israel as a marriage. Hence, credible evidence exists for believing that God, at creation, designed marriage to be a covenant relationship. Now I will turn to passages in the New Testament that support the covenantal nature of marriage as well.

Because the expression "covenant marriage" is absent in the New Testament, proving the covenantal nature of marriage proves more difficult. I demonstrated earlier, however, that lack of the precise term 'covenant' or phrase 'covenant marriage' does not necessarily preclude the presence of covenant marriage. Put another way, the reality can be present without the linguistic reference, even if the linguistic reference would make the reality much easier to prove. The method of approach for this section, therefore, will first demonstrate that New Testament authors could have spoken of marriage as a covenant without using the exact expression by means of inter-textuality—using compositional links. Second, New Testament passages will be identified and examined for evidence of covenant themes and links to passages confirming a covenant nature.

COMPOSITIONAL STRATEGIES

Modern biblical scholarship provides a growing number of tools for viewing Scripture, such as form criticism, source criticism, and redaction criticism.[23] One fairly new tool is compositional criticism, which George Fohrer describes as a powerful exegetical tool that seeks to explain the ways biblical writers composed literary units into a complete whole. Compositional criticism also attempts to understand the theological characteristics of both smaller and larger compositional units.[24] Using Fohrer's compositional criticism, Sailhamer examines the relationship between various biblical texts and observes how an author may compose a text using a strategy that makes up the whole fabric of biblical narrative books. Using this technique, he notes, one can begin to see how the Old and New Testaments relate.

Sailhamer labels the strategy of using various words, phrases, or ideas to link literary units into a literary whole inner-textuality. "By means of such links the biblical authors thematize their basic message."[25] For example, the links between the flood stories in Genesis and the purification laws in Leviticus beautifully illustrate how the author of the Pentateuch strategically composed his work, connecting what he wrote in Genesis with what he wrote in Leviticus.[26] Recognizing this inner-textuality, Sailhamer maintains, is imperative to interpreting accurately any passage.

While inner-textuality is the study of links within a single text, Sailhamer observes "inter-textuality is the study of links between and among texts. Many written texts, especially biblical ones, were written with the full awareness of other texts in mind."[27] Sailhamer states that biblical authors assumed readers would be thoroughly knowledgeable of those other texts. In addition, if an authorially intended inter-textuality exists, "then it stands to reason that some loss of meaning occurs when one fails to view the text in terms of it."[28] Lastly, Sailhamer argues that in an inter-textual approach, later canonical texts are understood as an explication and elaboration of earlier texts, with both the meaning of the earlier text and the meaning of the later text being maintained. The meaning of an earlier text becomes an assumed part of the later text.[29] Hans Frei similarly writes:

> The interpretive means for joining [biblical texts] was to make earlier biblical stories figures or types of later stories and of their events and patterns of meaning. Without loss to its own literal meaning or specific temporal reference, an earlier story (or occurrence) was to show that Old Testament persons, events, and prophecies were fulfilled in the New Testament. It was a way of turning the variety of biblical books into a single, unitary canon, one that embraced in particular the differences between Old and New Testaments. Far from being in conflict with the literal sense of biblical stories, figuration or typology was a natural extension of literal interpretation. It was literalism at the level of the whole biblical story and thus of the depiction of the whole of historical reality.[30]

Thus, later biblical texts can be understood properly only in light of their dependence on earlier texts which biblical authors strategically used during composition. In the next section I will put forth evidence that New Testament writers inter-textually linked their works to the Pentateuch and, in particular, that the authors of Ephesians and Matthew linked their discussions of marriage to the first chapters of Genesis.

COMPOSITIONAL LINKS TO THE PENTATEUCH

In his commentary on Ephesians, J. P. Sampley identifies an example of inter-textuality which he believes helps explain the relationship between husbands and wives. Since Ephesians 5:21–33 deals with the husband-wife relationship, Sampley is not surprised by the inclusion of Genesis 2:24, Scripture's primary passage regarding marriage. Nevertheless, Sampley addresses why the author introduced an Old Testament quotation at all. The answer, he reasons, lies in "an early Christian conventional formulation."[31]

Sampley identifies within the New Testament an early Christian formulation, which includes two elements: (1) a statement concerning a wife's submission using the Greek verb ὑποτάσσομαι and (2) a reference to the Torah for support.[32] 1 Timothy 2:8–15, for example, follows this pattern. After speaking to men in verse eight, the author writes, "Let a woman learn in silence with all submission [ὑποταγῃ]. And I do not permit a woman to teach or to have authority over a man, but to be in silence. For Adam was formed first, then Eve. And Adam was not deceived, but the woman being deceived, fell into transgression" (1 Tim 2:11–14). Addressing the husband-wife relationship, 1 Timothy refers to two aspects of the Genesis narrative, both of which serve to confirm the wife's submission to her husband. First, the author appeals to Adam's temporal priority to support the husband's authority. Secondly, the author notes that Eve, not Adam, was deceived. Hence, 1 Timothy illustrates this early Christian formulation.

Sampley similarly recognizes this pattern in 1 Corinthians 14:33–34, which states, "Let your women keep silent in the churches, for they are not permitted to speak; but *they are* to be submissive [ὑποτασσέσθωσαν], as the law also says." Again, the husband-wife relationship is considered by reference to the law, which Sampley contends is the Torah. Sampley observes this pattern also in 2 Corinthians 11:2–3 and 1 Peter 3:1–6 and concludes, "Each of these passages manifests a widespread early Christian convention of a reference to the pentateuch [sic] pattern or lesson to be applied to the understanding of the position of women in marriage in early Christian times."[33]

Like Sailhamer and Frei, Sampley detected a common compositional strategy whereby later biblical texts referred to earlier texts. As noted earlier, when an authorially-intended link between two texts exists, failure to recognize or observe this link results in misunderstanding the passage. This later reference in canonical texts is understood as an "explication and elaboration of earlier texts, with both the meaning of the earlier text and the meaning of the later text being maintained. The meaning of an earlier text becomes an assumed part of that of the later text."[34] Therefore, having shown that the Pentateuch understands the husband-wife relationship as covenant marriage, subsequent textual appeals to the relationship grounded in the Genesis narrative may reasonably be interpreted as references to marriage as a covenant relationship as well.

Because the expression "covenant marriage" is not used in the New Testament, demonstrating New Testament writers understood marriage as covenant proves more difficult. Nevertheless, an examination of selected passages from the New Testament will suffice that its authors not only understood marriage as covenant but also described the relationship using textual links to the Genesis narrative.

EPHESIANS 5:21–33

In addition to the challenge of interpreting the compositional link to Genesis, Ephesians 5:21–33 poses numerous interpretative difficulties, not the least of which pertains to the husband-wife relationship. For example, the precise reference of "mystery [μυστήριον]" in verse thirty-two is debated. Whereas Mitton and various Catholic scholars hold 'mystery' refers to marriage, which led to the identification of marriage as a sacrement by the Catholic Church,[35] other theologians maintain 'mystery' indicates the Christ-church relationship.[36] In like manner, scholars debate the scope of verse thirty-one and the "one flesh" union.

Fortunately, these points of contention do not detract from the overwhelming evidence supporting the understanding in this passage of marriage as a covenant. First, despite the lack of unanimity, the majority of commentators agree that the primary purpose of this pericope concerns the marriage institution. Goodspeed wrongly asserts this passage is not so much about marriage as it is "a glorious parable of the mystic union between Christ and the Church. . . . As we read the paragraph (5:22–33) we come to perceive that the writer is not so much exalting the marriage relation by comparing it to the union of Christ and the Church, as illuminating and adorning that doctrine by entwining it with the most familiar, intimate, and fruitful of human relations."[37] Similarly, Chavasse states the primary concern of this passage is not human marriages, but rather how it reflects the one great Marriage.[38]

Alternatively, most interpreters concur human marriage is the author's chief concern in Ephesians 5. Lincoln observes, "This passage begins and ends with exhortations to husbands and wives; it is part of the household code; and it is in the midst of the letter's serious paraenesis about believers' behavior in the world."[39] In the passage immediately preceding the pericope under question, Paul exhorts believers to "walk worthy of the calling . . . till we all come to the unity of the faith and of the knowledge of the Son of God, to a perfect man, to the measure of the stature of the fullness of God" (Eph. 4:1, 13). Paul is convinced that if one lives his life in this manner, it will be evident to the watching world, like replacing old clothes with new ones (Eph. 4:22–24). Thus, Paul makes his statements on marriage within the context of living the new, Spirit-filled life, a life noticeably different from the past. Consider how Paul uses the Christ-church relationship to illustrate this changed life in the husband-wife relationship. Dividing the text into two columns clearly illustrates the interplay between human marriage and the Christ-church relationship.[40]

Column A	**Column B**
22 Wives, submit to your own husbands, as to the Lord. 23 For the husband is head of the wife,	As [ὡς] also Christ is head of the church; and He is the Savior of the body. 24 Therefore, just as the church is subject to Christ,
so [οὕτως]*let* the wives *be* to their own husbands in everything. 25 Husbands, love your wives,	just as [καθὼς]Christ also loved the church and gave Himself for her, 26 that He might sanctify and cleanse her with the washing of water by the word, 27 that He might present her to Himself a glorious church, not having spot or wrinkle or any such thing, but that she should be holy and without blemish.
28 So [οὕτως] husbands ought to love their own wives as their own bodies; he who loves his wife loves himself. 29 For no one ever hated his own flesh, but nourishes and cherishes it,	just as [καθὼς] the Lord *does* the church. 30 For we are members of His body, of His flesh and of His bones.

31 "For this reason a man shall leave his father and mother and be joined to his wife, and the two shall become one flesh." 32 This is a great mystery,

	but I speak concerning Christ and the church.
33 Nevertheless [πλήν] let each one of you in particular so love his own wife as himself, and let the wife *see* that she respects *her* husband.	

Column A deals with the relationship between husbands and wives, and column B deals with the relation of Christ and the church. Note further that the columns are separated by *comparative* particles, thus presupposing some essential interrelationship.[41] Therefore, Paul discusses the husband-wife relationship in 22–23a and the description is supported by exposition of the Christ-church relationship in verses 23b–24a. Likewise, the husband-wife relationship in 24b–25a is illumined by the relationship espoused by Christ and the church in 25b–27. Lastly, the two relationships are brought together in verses 31–32 by a direct quote from Genesis 2:24. Hence, the primary purpose of Ephesians 5:21–33 is human marriage as it is illumined by the Christ-church relationship.

A second reason for understanding Ephesians 5 as supporting covenant marriage is its application of the early Christian formulation, what Sailhamer calls inter-textuality. As stated above, biblical writers often used compositional strategies—common terms, phrases, or events—to link later biblical texts to earlier texts. Later references are understood as explications and elaborations of earlier texts, with the meanings of both texts maintained. Various New Testament passages addressing the husband-wife relationship find the basis of their support in the Pentateuch, such as 1 Timothy 2, 2 Corinthians 11, 1 Corinthians 14, and 1 Peter 3. Ephesians 5 clearly follows this format, speaking to the husband-wife relationship in verses twenty-one to thirty and quoting Genesis 2:24. Ephesians, moreover, uniquely expands the quote's reference. That is, one is not surprised that Genesis 2:24 would be employed in a discussion on the relationship between husbands and wives, but Ephesians equally applies this verse to the Christ-church relationship: ἐγὼ δὲ λέγω εἰς Χριστὸν καὶ εἰς τὴν ἐκκλησίαν (Eph 5:32b).[42]

Sampley rightly insists that the author of Ephesians relates the accounts of Adam and Eve to the relationship of marriage partners to support his argument regarding submission. The Ephesians passage does more, however. By appealing to Genesis, a passage that earlier was shown to view marriage as covenant, the author utilizes a compositional strategy linking Genesis' understanding to the current passage. This inter-textual link suggests Ephesians 5:21–33 should also be interpreted as identifying marriage as a covenant.

A third reason for understanding Ephesians 5 as a passage that supports identifying marriage as a covenant, and a reason that substantiates the above argument, is Ephesians 5 also alludes to Ezekiel 16, another Old Testament passage that identifies marriage as a covenant. In Ezekiel 16, Yahweh passes by a young Jerusalem and finds her "at the age of love" (Ezk 16:8). As a result, Yahweh entered a covenant relationship with Jerusalem, a relationship that is clearly identified as marriage. Following this covenant marriage, the text reads, "Then I washed you in water; yes, I thoroughly washed off your blood, and I anointed you with oil" (Ezk 16:9). In both Ezekiel and Ephesians, the washing with water is connected with the husband purifying his wife.[43] Therefore, bathing imagery connects the covenant understanding of marriage in Ezekiel with the husband-wife relationship in Ephesians 5:21–33. And hence, O'Brien correctly concludes:

> Christ and the church in a loving relationship is the paradigm for the Christian husband and wife. . . . This particular view of marriage has its antecedents in the Old Testament, where marriage is used typologically of the relationship between God and his covenant people. In the earlier Testament the image of marriage was often used to depict the covenant relationship between Yahweh and his people, Israel. Jesus took over this teaching and boldly referred to himself as the Bridegroom (Mk 2:18–20; John 3:29). He presented 'himself in the role of Yahweh in the divine marriage with the covenanted people. Paul expands on the image in 2 Corinthians 11:1–3 and here in Ephesians 5, and focuses particularly on 'the sacrificial steadfastness of the heavenly 'Bridegroom's covenant-love for his bride.' At one level, then, Paul's teaching on marriage is grounded in the Old Testament, while at another level the church's marriage to Christ is prefigured in Adam and Eve.[44]

By recognizing that the primary focus of Ephesians 5:21–33 is the human, marriage relationship and by linking it inter-textually with Old Testament passages that speak of marriage as covenant, one may conclude the author of Ephesians must also understand marriage as a covenant institution.

MATTHEW 19:1–10 (MARK 10:1–12)

Matthew 19:1–10, and its parallel passage in Mark 10:1–12, constitutes a second New Testament passage addressing the nature and meaning of marriage. Like the Ephesians pericope, the term "covenant marriage" is conspicuously absent. Nevertheless, sufficient evidence exists for viewing Matthew's understanding of marriage as being significantly dependent upon marriage as a covenant institution.

First, Matthew inter-textually links Jesus' statement on marriage to Genesis 2:24. Jesus says:

> Have you not read that He who made *them* at the beginning 'made them male and female,' and said, 'For this reason a man shall leave his father and mother and be joined to his wife, and the two shall become one flesh'? So then, they are no longer two but one flesh. Therefore what God has joined together, let not man separate" (Matt 19:4–6).

This authorial connection to Genesis 2, which identifies marriage as covenant, demonstrates Jesus understood marriage as a covenant instituted by God. Mistakenly, some scholars fail to see this connection to covenant marriage in the New Testament. Accordingly, Eugene Roop asserts, "The texts which we usually use from the New Testament [concerning marriage] are not involved in the question of covenant, violation, judgment, or new covenant . . . They take as their focus of concern the ongoing Jewish debate about the adequate grounds for divorce, a debate that is not present in the Old Testament."[45] Thus, because marriage in the New Testament is often framed within a discussion concerning divorce rather than an explicit reference to covenant, Roop contends the concept of covenant marriage is absent from the New Testament.

Conversely, because the New Testament insists on speaking about marriage within the context of divorce, marriage ought to be seen covenantally (Matt 5:27–33; Matt 19:1–10; Mark 10:1–12; and 1 Cor 7:1–16). This second major reason for identifying marriage as a covenant in Matthew is based upon its parallel with the majority of passages used to support the idea of marriage as covenant in the Old Testament. Jesus' statements concerning marriage and divorce in Matthew are significantly similar to reports found in Malachi 2. Both passages make reference to God's creation of humanity and the one flesh union.[46] Smith paraphrases Malachi 2:15, "Did not he (God) make one . . . therefore a man leaves his father and mother and cleaves to his wife, and the two become one flesh."[47] Hence, Davies and Allison confidently write "This sets Malachi's criticism of divorce squarely beside the same two verses quoted in the gospels."[48] By observing that Malachi and Matthew quote the same verses, one may reasonably argue Matthew was cognizant of Malachi when the text was being composed.

Malachi and Matthew reach beyond citing identical passages. We find within Malachi's discussion of marriage are both (1) a reference to its covenantal nature, which is supported by an inter-textual link to Genesis 2; (2) and a reference to God's strong abhorrence of divorce (Mal 2:16). In a similar fashion, Jesus also references Genesis 2 and immediately draws a connection with the immorality of divorce: "What God has joined together, let not man separate" (Matt 19:6).

Surprisingly, all commentators have failed to notice this same pattern exists for other passages in the Old Testament that speak of marriage as a covenant. Proverbs, for instance, warns the one "who forsakes the companion of her youth and forgets the covenant of her God" (Pro 2:17). In similar fashion, the verse may read of "who has left her partner," and thus, be likened to divorce. Thus, one again sees the relation of marriage as covenant connected with discussions of divorce, forsaking, and abandoning one's spouse. One may reasonably deduce covenant marriage is marked by permanence and faithful commitment. Hosea beautifully illustrates each of these components. Roop, therefore, was correct when he wrote, "One has to say that when the New Testament interprets marriage as a covenant, i.e., permanent relationship, established by God, this is an interpretation not inconsistent with the intention of Genesis 2 in its own context."[49] By recognizing Matthew's compositional link to Genesis and his parallels with other Old Testament, covenant passages, one may reasonably conclude Matthew also identified marriage as a covenant relationship.

SUMMARY

In this chapter I have sought to demonstrate the essential covenant nature of marriage established in the first two chapters of Genesis is reaffirmed by passages in subsequent Scripture. In the Old Testament, the books of Hosea, Proverbs, and Ezekiel reinforce the idea of covenant marriage by metaphorically describing the covenant relationship between God and Israel as a marriage. In the New Testament, Ephesians, Matthew, and Mark inter-textually link their discussions of the husband-wife relationship to Old Testament passages identifying marriage as covenant. Most emphatically, Matthew's treatment of marriage parallels several Old Testament passages regarding covenant marriage by discussing marriage within the context of God's abhorrence for divorce and his original intentions for a "one flesh" union. Marriage, therefore, may reasonably be understood as a covenant instituted by God.

NOTES

1. For a discussion of the purpose of Hosea, see Douglas Stuart, *Hosea-Jonah*, Word Biblical Commentary, no. 31, ed. David A. Hubbard and Glenn W. Barker (Nashville: Thomas Nelson Publishers, 1987), 47. Here, Stuart notes the purpose of Hosea 2 is corrective and restorative. "Ultimately, the plaintiff does not so much seek a divorce as a chastened wife." This interpretation also supports the unconditional nature of a covenant. Since covenants are

established, witnessed, and guaranteed by God, they are dependent upon his will and authority. Consequently, the covenant depends on the faithfulness of God and not the fidelity of the covenanting parties.

2. See Gale A. Yee, *Composition and Tradition in the Book of Hosea: A Redaction Critical Investigation* (Atlanta: Scholars Press, 1987), 105–8. Yee's work contains several positive contributions to studies in Hosea. However, his reconstruction of the history of Hosea provides more innovation than clarification. For example, he writes that the original adulterous woman described in chapter two is Rachel, the wife of Jacob, rather than Gomer.

3. Gordon Paul Hugenberger, *Marriage As a Covenant: A Study of Biblical Law and Ethics Governing Marriage Developed From the Perspective of Malachi* (Leiden: E. J. Brill, 1994), 216–79.

4. See Hans Walter Wolff, *Hosea. A Commentary on the Book of the Prophet Hosea*, Hermeneia (Philadelphia: Fortress Press, 1974), 33; U. Cassuto, "Second Chapter of the Book of Hosea, " in U. Cassuto, *Biblical and Oriental Studies*, (Jerusalem: Magnes, 1973), 120–122.

5. For arguments against identifying Hosea 2:4 with Near Eastern divorce formulae, see Yee, *Composition and Tradition in the Book of Hosea*, 105.

6. Fritsch and Schloerb express the traditional argument best, stating: "The marriage relationship is described as a covenant entered into by divine sanction. It is a serious matter which should not easily be forgotten, certainly not broken." Charles T. Fritsch and Rolland Schloerb, *The Book of* Proverbs, The Interpreter's Bible, no. 4, ed. George Arthur Buttrick (Nashville: Abingdon Press, 1955), 796.

7. For an excellent survey of possible interpretations for the "strange woman," see Michael V. Fox, Proverbs *1–9*, in *The Anchor Bible*, ed. William Foxwell Albright and David Noel Freedman (New York: Doubleday, 2000), 135–141. See also James G. Williams, *Women Recounted: Narrative Thinking and the God of Israel*, Bible and Literature Series, ed. David M. Gunn (Sheffield: Almond Press, 1982), 107–10.

8. See Hugenberger, *Marriage as a Covenant*, 297.

9. Ibid.

10. See William McKane, *Proverbs: A New Approach* (Philadelphia: Westminster Press, 1970), 285. See also Fox, *Proverbs 1–9*, 914.

11. Crawford H. Toy, *A Critical and Exegetical Commentary on the Book of Proverbs*, The International Critical Commentary, ed. Samuel Rolles Driver, Alfred Plummer and Charles Briggs (New York: Charles Scribner's Sons, 1899), 46. Also, see Hugenberger, *Marriage as a Covenant*, 297.

12. Roland E. Murhpy, *Proverbs*, Word Biblical Commentary, no. 22, ed. Bruce M. Metzger, David A. Hubbard and Glenn W. Barker (Nashville: Thomas Nelson Publishers, 1998), 16.

13. See Derek Kidner, *Proverbs: An Introduction and Commentary*, Tyndale Old Testament Commentaries (Downers Grove: InterVarsity Press, 1964), 62.

14. See Claudia V. Camp, *Wisdom and the Feminine in the Book of Proverbs*, Bible and Literature Series, no. 11 (Sheffield, England: Almond

Press, 1985), 235–71. Also, see Hugenberger, *Marriage as a Covenant*, 299–302.

15. See Moshe Greenberg, *Ezekiel 1–20*, Anchor Bible, no. 22, ed. William Foxwell Albright and David Noel Freedman (Garden City, NY: Doubleday and Company, 1983), 273–306.

16. See Walther Eichrodt, *Ezekiel: A Commentary*, 2d ed., The Old Testament Library, ed. G. Ernest Wright et al., trans. Cosslett Quin (Philadelphia: Westminster Press, 1975), 201–20. For similar interpretations, see also John W. Wevers, *Ezekiel*, Century Bible (Copewood, NJ: Thomas Nelson and Sons, 1969); and Walther Zimmerli, *Ezekiel 1–24*, Hermeneia: A Critical and Historical Commentary on the Bible, ed. Frank Moore Cross et al., trans. Ronald E. Clements (Philadelphia: Fortress Press, 1979).

17. See Greenberg, *Ezekiel 1–20*, 277–8; Leslie C. Allen, *Ezekiel 1–19*, Word Biblical Commentary, no. 28, ed. David A. Hubbard and Glenn W. Barker (Dallas: Word Books, 1994), 238; G. A. Cooke, *A Critical and Exegetical Commentary on the Book of Ezekiel*, in *International Critical Commentary* (Edinburgh: T. & T. Clark, 1951), 163; Eichrodt, *Ezekiel*, 205–6; Wevers, *Ezekiel*, 121; and Zimmerli, *Ezekiel 1–24*, 339–40.

18. Hugenberger, *Marriage as a Covenant*, 304.

19. Allen, *Ezekiel 1–19*, 238.

20. See Wevers, *Ezekiel*, 121.

21. John Calvin, *Commentaries on the First Twenty Chapters of the Book of The Prophet Ezekiel*, trans. Thomas Myers (Grand Rapids: William B. Eerdmans Publishing Company, 1948), 104. See also Greenberg, *Ezekiel 1–20*, 278.

22. See Hugenberger, *Marriage as a Covenant*, 306–7.

23. For a discussion concerning these various tools, see John H. Sailhamer, *Introduction to Old Testament Theology: A Canonical Approach* (Grand Rapids: Zondervan Publishing Company, 1995), 88–103.

24. See George Fohrer, Exegese Des Alten Testaments: Einfuhrung in Die Methodik (Quelle and Myer, 1983), 142.

25. See also Sailhamer, *Introduction to Old Testament Theology*, 98 and 209–10.

26. For an illustration of the inner-textuality in this passage, see John H. Sailhamer, *The Pentateuch As Narrative* (Grand Rapids: Zondervan Publishing Company, 1992), 358–59.

27. Sailhamer, *Introduction to Old Testament Theology*, 212–3.

28. Ibid.

29. Ibid., 95.

30. Hans Frei, *The Eclipse of Biblical Narrative: A Study in Eighteenth and Nineteenth Century Biblical Narrative* (New Haven: Yale University Press, 1974), 1–4. See also Erich Auerbach, *Mimesis: The Representation of Reality in Western Literature* (Princeton: Princeton University Press, 1953), 12.

31. J. Paul Sampley, '*And the Two Shall Become One Flesh': A Study of Traditions in Ephesians 5:21–33* (Cambridge: Cambridge University Press, 1971), 96–7.

32. See Ibid., 97.
33. Ibid., 99.
34. Sailhamer, *Introduction to Old Testament Theology*, 95.
35. See C. Leslie Mitton, *Ephesians*, New Century Bible, ed. Ronald E. Clements and Matthew Black (London: Oliphants, 1976), 207–8. For a discussion of others who have understood "mystery" to refer to marriage, see T. K. Abbott, *A Critical and Exegetical Commentary on The Epistles to the Ephesians and to the Colossians*, International Critical Commentary, ed. Charles Augustus Briggs, Samuel Rolles Driver and Alfred Plummer (New York: Charles Scribner's Sons, 1897), 174–5; Andrew T. Lincoln, *Ephesians*, Word Biblical Commentary, no. 42, ed. David A. Hubbard and Glenn W. Barker (Dallas: Word Books, 1990), 380–1; and Peter T. O'Brien, *The Letter to the Ephesians*, The Pillar New Testament Commentary, ed. D. A. Carson (Grand Rapids: William B. Eerdmans Publishing Company, 1999), 430–1.
36. See Charles Hodge, *A Commentary on the Epistle to the Ephesians* (Grand Rapids: William B. Eerdmans Publishing Company, 1950), 351; and Andreas J. Kostenberger, "The Mystery of Christ and the Church: Head and Body, 'One Flesh'," *Trinity Journal* 12 (1991): 86–7.
37. Edgar J. Goodspeed, *The Meaning of Ephesians* (Chicago: University of Chicago Press, 1933), 61–2.
38. See Claude Chavasse, The Bride of Christ: An Enquiry Into the Nuptial Element in Early Christianity (London: Faber and Faber, 1940), 77.
39. Lincoln, *Ephesians*, 353.
40. The following chart is adapted from Sampley, *'And the Two Shall Become One'*, 104.
41. See Ibid., 107.
42. See also Ibid., 100.
43. See Zimmerli, *Ezekiel 1–24*, 351; Hodge, *Ephesians*, 318; Lincoln, *Ephesians*, 363, 387; and Sampley, *'And the Two Shall Become One'*, 40–3.
44. O'Brien, *The Letter to the Ephesians*, 433, 435.
45. Eugene Roop, "Two Become One Become Two," *Brethern Life and Thought* 21 (1976): 136.
46. See Hugenberger, *Marriage as a Covenant*, 124–51.
47. Ralph L. Smith, *Micah-Malachi*, Word Biblical Commentary (Waco: Word Books, 1984), 324.
48. W. D. Davies and Dale C. Allison, *The Gospel According to Saint Matthew*, The International Critical Commentary on the Holy Scriptures of the Old and New Testaments, ed. J. A. Emerton, C. E. B. Cranfield and G. N. Stanton (Edinburgh: T. & T. Clark, 1997), 12.
49. Roop, "Two become One become Two," 135.

Chapter 6

Theological and Moral Implications of the Covenant Marriage

In previous chapters I have put forth evidence that God, at creation, designed marriage to be a covenant relationship. After using a biblical-concept approach to define covenant, I presented arguments from Genesis and Malachi supporting the covenant nature of marriage from the beginning. In chapter five, I showed that subsequent passages in Scripture dealing with marriage are consistent with this interpretation as well. Based upon this evidence, I concluded that marriage was instituted by God as a covenant at creation. Now, in this final chapter, I will focus on what this implies. How should believing God made marriage to be a covenant relationship affect the way one understands the moral boundaries surrounding the marriage relationship? If biblical marriage is a covenant, then its covenant nature must shed special insight on the value and significance of moral standards God says should govern the practice of human marriage. After delineating eight theological truths that emerge from the covenant nature of marriage, I will examine some of the resulting moral implications.

THEOLOGICAL OBSERVATIONS

God Establishes Covenant Marriage

First, God establishes covenant marriage. God is sovereign, Creator of all that is good. The creation of marriage is no exception. To the church at Colossae, the apostle Paul writes, "For by Him all things were created that are in heaven and that are on earth, visible and invisible, whether thrones or dominions or principalities or powers. All things were created through him and for him" (Col 1:16). Thus, Paul not only suggests that Christ created all things, but that they were created for his pleasure.

The author of Genesis depicts a loving God who, upon recognizing that it was not good for man to be alone, fashioned Eve and brought her to Adam (Gen 2:22). Later, Malachi records that the Lord made them one flesh, emphasizing both the covenant nature of marriage and the establishment of it at creation (Mal 2:15). In his discussion with the Pharisees concerning divorce, Jesus alludes to the Father's establishment of marriage as well: "Have you not read that He who made them at the beginning 'made them male and female,' and said, 'For this reason a man shall leave his father and mother and be joined to his wife, and the two shall become one flesh'" (Matt 19:4–5; see also Mark 10:6–9). Thus, Jesus says God made marriage. Therefore, God clearly designs and establishes covenant marriage, even for his good pleasure.

Marriage is Fundamentally Covenantal

Second, because God made marriage a covenant from the start, being a covenant is *essential* to the basic meaning of marriage. From the beginning, God consciously designed certain orders as a basis for knowing and understanding his will. As a result, these orders are universal and necessarily binding on all creatures, for all times, and in all cultures. Walter Kaiser states "These ordinances reflect the work of God in creation and depict 'the constitution of things' as they were intended to be from the Creator's hand. They cover and regulate the whole gamut of life."[1] Therefore, because God designed marriage to be a covenant relationship in the beginning, it is not only important, but also essential to the meaning of marriage and necessarily binding on humankind.

God Enforces Covenant Marriage

Third, not only does God establish covenant marriage, God also enforces and bears witness to it. A number of covenant passages, such as the stories of Laban and Jacob and the stories of Jonathan and David, include reference to a witness (Gen 31:55 and 1 Sam 20:16). "Since God was a witness to the agreements between the men," Elliot writes, "their agreement was in essence a pledge to God."[2] Each participant in the covenant swore to God to be faithful to the terms of the covenant and, in addition, invoked God to respond against any breach of the covenant.[3] By identifying God as the "witness" to the covenant, both parties recognized God as the one who enforces and validates the covenant's conditions. God is not merely the one who punishes offenders, although he does, but more importantly, he authorizes the covenant. God is viewed, according to Scripture, as the one who guarantees the covenant stipulations.[4] Hence, Malachi exclaims, "The Lord is witness between you and the wife of your youth" (Mal 2:15). Because covenant marriage is established by oath and has God as its witness, it depends on his will and authority.

Obligations in Covenant Marriage are Moral

Fourth, obligations in covenant marriage are moral. Marriage is more than a social or legal relationship. Because marriage is a covenant relationship, it is established by and accountable to God, who is the supreme Moral Ruler of the Universe. Consequently, the obligations in the marriage relationship are moral.

Not only are obligations in marriage moral, the scale on which God weighs the satisfaction of marriage obligations is his holiness: "I am the Lord who brought you up out of Egypt to be your God; therefore be holy, because I am holy" (Lev 11:45).5 God weighs everything that one does against the backdrop of his holiness. Because God is holy, one is to walk after him and also be holy. "No one is holy like the Lord, for there is none besides You, nor is there any rock like our God. . . . And by Him actions are weighed" (1 Sam 2:2–3). The psalmist similarly proclaims, "Blessed is the man who walks not in the counsel of the ungodly, nor stands in the path of sinners, nor sits in the seat of the scornful; But his delight is in the law of the Lord, and in His law he meditates day and night" (Ps 1:1–2). Holiness touches every aspect of life: worship, family, wealth, and marriage.

The Old Testament Holiness Code demonstrates that holiness penetrates every facet of life (Lev 18–20). The Levitical author discusses holiness in sexual behavior, in social ethics, in worship, and in marriage and family relations. The author of Hebrews links holiness to marriage as well: "Marriage is honorable among all, and the bed undefiled; but fornicators and adulterers God will judge" (Heb 13:4). Nowhere, however, is this link more emphatic than in Paul's charge to husbands and wives. "Husbands, love your wives, just as Christ also loved the Church and gave himself for her, that he might sanctify and cleanse her with the washing of water by the word, that he might present her to himself a glorious Church, not having spot or wrinkle or any such thing, but that she should be holy and without blemish" (Eph 5:25–27).

The key to understanding how holiness relates to marriage hinges on Paul's phrase, "just as." Paul not only says a husband must love his wife, but that his love should reflect Christ's love for the Church. Christ's love for the Church is a purifying and cleansing love. Christ's love for the Church permits him to present her without blemish before the Father. Likewise, Paul says a husband's love toward his wife should cultivate purity. Just as God demands moral holiness in his relations to the Church, so he demands moral holiness in covenant marriage. Obligations in marriage are moral because they are enforced by and accountable to God alone.

Obligations in Covenant Marriage are Unconditional

Fifth, obligations in covenant marriage are unconditional. When Israel failed to live faithfully according to the terms of her covenant with God, the Lord graciously responded "Nevertheless I will remember my covenant with you in the days of your youth, and I will establish an everlasting covenant with you" (Ezek 16:59–60). Even when Israel played the role of the harlot and the terms of the covenant had been broken, God remained faithful to his covenant with Israel. The Lord's actions concerning covenant responsibility intimate that the obligations of a covenant, including marriage, are unconditional.

Malachi also suggests the obligations of covenant marriage are unconditional. After he describes the husband as "dealing treacherously" with his wife by violating the covenant of marriage, Malachi contends she is still "the wife of your youth" and "your wife by covenant" (Mal 2:14). Like the covenant passages in Ezekiel, Malachi maintains the unconditional nature of covenant obligations, especially in marriage. As a result, obligations in marriage are not dependent upon the behavior of either party. Since the obligations of covenant marriage are set by God, and because the obligations in covenant marriage are moral and accountable to God who enforces the terms of the marriage, they are clearly unconditional. Man does not possess the authority to alter what God fixed at creation—namely, the terms of covenant marriage.

Covenant Marriage is Secured by One's Life

Sixth, not only are the obligations of marriage moral and unconditional, but covenant marriage itself is secured by one's life. Few expressions illustrate the seriousness of covenant marriage more than Malachi's warning, "Take heed of your life" (Mal 2:15–16). The Lord expects those who enter covenant marriage to remain faithful to its terms, and hints that failure to carry out fully its provisions threatens one's very existence.

Other scriptural passages reflect this same perspective. For example, the writer of Proverbs associates blessings and curses with one's faithfulness to covenant obligations, including death for an adulterous wife (Pro 2:18: Compare with Deut 30:19). Many covenants were often signified by blood sacrifice, including the New Covenant, which depicts the serious nature of keeping the covenant (Matt 26:27). As covenant participants, marriage partners pledge their lives and service: "till death do us part."

Covenant Marriage Arises from being Made Male and Female in the Image of God for One Flesh Union

The Gospel of Matthew records, "Have you not read that He who made them at the beginning 'made them male and female,' and said, 'For this reason a man shall leave his father and mother and be joined to his wife, and the two shall become one flesh'" (Matt 19:4–5). A logical connection exists between the fact that God "made them male and female," and the fact that "the two shall become one flesh." One cannot separate a discussion of sexuality from a discussion on the theology of marriage. Marriage, regardless of how it is defined, is between two individuals, individuals who must be either male or female.

God designed humanity with the possibility of confrontation, similar to the relationship that exists within God himself.[6] Just as God confronts humanity in an I-Thou relationship, so also man has the capacity for this same relationship. Humanity is created for relationship with God and with fellow humans, including marriage. The author of Genesis, under the inspiration of God, records the creation of humanity as male and female immediately prior to his elaboration of covenant marriage. Scripture closely relates these two ideas: being created male and female and being created for covenant marriage—one flesh union. Malachi likewise echoes the teachings of Genesis when he asks, "Has not the Lord made them one?" According to Genesis, Malachi, and Jesus himself, covenant marriage rests on what it means to be made male and female in the image of God for one flesh union.

Covenant Marriage Places Primary Responsibility on the Husband

In addition to the above theological assertions related to covenant marriage, God also designed it with the primary responsibility ascribed to the husband. Chapter two acknowledged the frequency with which familial and social relationships supplied the paradigm for covenant obligations, such as "brother," "father," "son," and "lord."[7] Beside the terms "brother," "father," and "son," however, no familial relationship designates covenanting parties more often than the husband-wife analogy. Examples abound in Isaiah, Jeremiah, Ezekiel, and in Hosea.

Interconnected with each of these models, Hugenberger writes, "is the pre-eminent covenantal obligation of 'love' [אהב]."[8] Scripture places the primary responsibility of obedient love on the husband. For example, the second chapters of both Genesis and Malachi stress the husband's duty to love his wife and not the wife's duty toward her husband, as might be expected (see Gen 2:24 and Mal 2:14). Whereas Scripture clearly instructs wives to love their husbands, a greater emphasis appears to be directed toward the husband (Titus 2:4):

> An obligation of nurture and love on Adam's part is already implied in the mode of Eve's creation as well as in Adam's recognition of Eve as "bone of my bones and flesh of my flesh." Removing any doubt concerning this pre-eminent obligation, however, the narrator concludes in Gen. 2:24 that a man should "leave his father and his mother" and "cleave to his wife, and they will become one flesh." The greatest and most enduring natural love and loyalty which a man once owed to his parents is now to be superseded by an even greater love and loyalty to his wife.[9]

Hence, Scripture clearly places the primary responsibility on the husband to love his wife in covenant marriage.

Conclusion

Thus far, the purpose of this study in biblical and theological ethics has been to explore Scripture's teaching concerning covenant marriage. Earlier chapters proved that God, at creation, designed marriage to be a covenant relationship. This chapter seeks to delineate corresponding theological truths, which in turn, set the stage for the following discussion of moral implications. Based upon work in previous chapters, eight theological comments are appropriate. Scripture affirms God established covenant marriage and continues to serve as its enforcing authority. Because God designed marriage at creation as a covenant relationship, moreover, the concept of covenant is essential to its basic meaning. Since covenant marriage is accountable to God, its obligations are moral and unconditional, even secured by one's life and service. Lastly, covenant marriage and all that it entails, rests on what it means to be made male and female in the image of God for one flesh union. The next section seeks to elucidate the moral consequences within covenant marriage that spring from these theological truths.

MORAL IMPLICATIONS

The heart of this chapter, building on the previous chapters' foundation, addresses the question: if God made marriage to be a covenant relationship, how must it affect the way one understands moral boundaries surrounding the marriage relationship? Specifically, the following discussion asserts that God, at creation, designed covenant marriage to be exclusive, heterosexual, fruitful, life-long, and ordered.

God Designed Covenant Marriage to be Exclusive

First, God designed covenant marriage to be an exclusive relationship. This exclusivity finds its basis in the idea of one flesh union. How is the Church to understand this mystical, one flesh union that exists between husband and wife? Theologically, what can the Church say about marriage, understanding it as a covenanted, one flesh union? In the first place, one flesh union reiterates the Hebrew understanding of viewing the body holistically. Hellenistic dualism, which separates humanity's existence into body and soul, and then, looks with disdain on what takes place in the body, is foreign to Scripture's view of man. Within Christianity, no dichotomy exists. Unlike paganism, Christianity teaches more than immortality of the soul; Christianity teaches resurrection of the body.[10] Indeed, what is done in the body matters. This understanding explains why it is wrong for a Christian to have sex with prostitutes; he unites his whole body, which belongs to the Lord, with one who does not belong to the Lord. He is uniting not only his outside body, which is created by God, but he is also joining his soul: tantamount to joining Christ Himself to a prostitute.[11]

Second, one flesh union by definition implies exclusivity. Certainly the term one is clear. It cannot refer to one at a time, but rather, must refer to the one with whom a covenant relationship has been offered, accepted, and sealed by sexual intercourse. The writer of Genesis characterizes the exclusiveness this way: "a man . . . and his wife" (Gen 2:24). The implication is clear; no other should be involved.

Here the words of Proverbs reverberate, "Drink water from your own cistern and running water from your own well" (Pro 5:15). Like *Yahweh's* relationship with Israel, the marriage relationship is to be exclusive. Thus, any overture to another is adultery. One cannot over emphasize this aspect. Israel committed spiritual "adultery" in many ways: idolatry, pagan worship, killing, and stealing, to name a few.[12] God considered Israel adulterous for expending energy on another that was supposed to be directed toward God alone. Likewise, one commits adultery in more ways than sexual intercourse. Adultery breaks the necessary exclusivity of the marriage relationship. Furthermore, adultery gives something to another that should be given only to the spouse: a touch, a look, or even oneself.

In a similar fashion, masturbation violates the marriage covenant. Marriage is a covenant relationship between two individuals. Masturbation, or self-stimulation, by definition is non-relational. Like adultery, it spends energy on self that should be directed toward one's spouse or future mate. As a result, it violates the holiness with which the Christian marriage must be measured. In the absence of a spouse, one risks lustful and adulterous fantasies, focusing on self, rather than the other. Finally, masturbation fails to meet either the unitive or the procreative purposes of sexuality, which were established at creation.[13]

In summary, God designed marriage to be a covenanted one flesh union, which encompasses a holistic view of man. Consequently, in the course of sexual intimacy, participants not only physically unite themselves to one another, but spiritually as well, equivalent to Christ's presence in the process. Accordingly, sexual intercourse with a prostitute violates covenant marriage, comparable to joining Christ with a prostitute. More fundamentally, one violates covenant marriage anytime he gives what alone should be reserved for his spouse, such as a look, a touch, or even oneself—adultery.

God Designed Covenant Marriage to be Heterosexual

Not only did God design covenant marriage to be exclusive, but he also intended it to be heterosexual. The Gospel of Matthew records, "Have you not read that He who made them at the beginning 'made them male and female,' and said, 'For this reason a man shall leave his father and mother and be joined to his wife, and the two shall become one flesh'" (Matt 19:4–5). Scripture intentionally connects God creating them "male and female," and commanding "the two shall become one flesh." One flesh union finds its basis in the concept of sexuality, what it means fundamentally to be made male and female. Biblical marriage is between two individuals, individuals who must be either male or female.

In his treatise, *The Estate of Marriage (1522)*, Luther comments on Genesis 1:27: "From this passage we may be assured that God divided mankind into two classes, namely, male and female, or a he and a she. This was so pleasing to him that he himself called it a good creation (Genesis 1:31)."[14] Thus, to some extent, sexuality is biologically related; God has made two varieties.

In *Sexual Ethics: An Evangelical Perspective*, Stanley Grenz notes sexuality refers to more than physical differences and reproduction.[15] One is male or female before the onset of puberty, as well as after the reproductive years. Hence, sexuality is more than a biological and psychological function. Again, Grenz recognizes "sexual distinction as being present already from the beginning with the creation of the woman from the man."[16]

The author of Genesis records "God created man in His own image; in the image of God He created him; male and female He created them" (Gen 1:27). In this creation account, God not only creates humanity in his image, but he creates them differently. Although man and woman both equally bear the image of God, a sexual duality exists.[17] Moreover, whatever God does, he does for a reason. Therefore, that there are sexual differences is significant, and a failure to recognize properly these differences, results in confusion of the sexes, confusion in marriage, and confusion in the church. Although the fall distorts these differences, they remain consistent with God's purpose. Hence, sexual difference, which results from God making two classes—male and female—affects the moral limits surrounding marriage. Consider German theologian Helmut Thielicke's contribution regarding sexuality.

Thielicke locates sexuality in two dimensions, how it relates to being and how it relates to function. For Thielicke, sexuality is part of the essential nature of being human, one's being. "By man in his *being* we mean man as he is related to God, man insofar as he is the bearer of responsibility and an infinite value and insofar as he thus has the dignity of being an 'end in himself' (Kant), that is, never to be used as a means to an end."[18] That is, in his being, man bears the image of God and has value merely as an aspect of creation.

Sexuality also includes one's function, which refers to "man as he actively steps out of himself, accomplishes and effects something, becomes, so to speak, 'productive'—whether it has to do with things or persons."[19] Distinct from being, function locates sexuality in not only who one is, but also in how one acts and relates to others. These two dimensions provide the framework for what it means essentially to be human. "When the two are isolated from each other the immediate and inevitable result is the emergence of pathological conditions of psychic or social kind."[20] That is, chaos results from failing to recognize the interconnectedness of being and function.

Thielicke illustrates how these elements have been skewed in history. For example, Karl Marx's critique of the capitalist society is that it has dehumanized people by its overemphasis on a person's productive capacities to the exclusion of the individual as a person. Indeed, the function a person performs appears most important in many capitalist societies. Hence, when one no longer produces, one has no value.

Within marriage, this over emphasis on the functionary purpose of the individual leads to valuing a woman only for her ability to reproduce or please one sexually, or to value a man only for his ability to provide for the family. Lewis Smedes notes, "Technique has replaced morality as the crucial question to ask about sex: technique in gaining the opportunity and technique in performance."[21] Therefore, when a spouse loses the ability to please the other or fulfill a predetermined functionary purpose, he or she may be disregarded and exchanged for another. To overemphasize function to the exclusion of being results in a degradation of the individual, a devaluing of a person made in the image of God, and leads to severing the marriage bond.

Likewise, overemphasizing a person's being to the exclusion of function causes a less than whole picture of the individual. Here, Thielicke reminds the reader of Goethe's poem, *Werther*, which stresses the importance of a being who is able to love and be loved. Thielicke asks, does "this Werther ha[ve] no function to perform (did he not have to have a student job or work as a candidate for a degree?) And, if he had been obliged to perform such functions, would he not have had far less trouble with his hypertrophied being and his love-sick sufferings and sorrows?"[22] Again, within marriage, to view a person only in terms of his being results in functional differences being either irrelevant or non-existent. Consequently, the church and society's structures will begin to fade.

Biblical marriage, therefore, rests on a proper understanding of sexuality. That humans are sexual beings is evident. Moreover, that sexuality involves more than biological differences is also evident. Failure to understand sexuality as both being and function skews one's understanding of the sexes and how each relates in the church, society, and within marriage; moral chaos results.

Scripture presents two major purposes of our sexuality, to unite and to generate. Following both creation accounts in Genesis, God enunciates the two purposes. First, he commands the couple to "Be fruitful and multiply" (Gen 1:28); Second, God says that "Therefore a man shall leave his father and mother and be joined to his wife, and they shall become one flesh" (Gen 2:24). Murray states that this revelation from God "gave meaning and purpose to the male and female composition of the race."[23] In his discussion with the Pharisees concerning divorce, Jesus linked these two creation mandates, procreation and unity.[24] God's purpose for creating male and female in his image, was that the two might unite, and hence, matrimony, and also that the two might reproduce, and therefore, fill the earth. This twofold purpose hinges on the need for sexual difference.

Stanley Grenz asserts God created Eve to be a savior, "another human being who would deliver Adam from his solitude by being a suitable bonding partner for him, not merely sexually, but in all dimensions of existence."[25] Similarly, Kaiser suggests that the theological understanding of creation is that God made for man a beautiful garden, animals to serve him, and a woman for companionship, concluding that loneliness was not good.[26] That this helper was created for more than companionship is made clear by how she differed from the rest of creation. Adam walked in the garden and spoke freely with God before the creation of Eve. Moreover, he had the companionship of the animals. Whatever companionship Eve brought Adam, therefore, it significantly differed from the relationship Adam shared with God and with the animals. "God creates woman not as the mirror image of man but as his counterpart, like him and yet unlike him. Because she is flesh of his flesh, they correspond to each other and are made for relation with each other; because she is not simply his mirror image, they can become 'one flesh.'"[27] In other words, God created a helper for companionship with man, but the significance of the creation is that she corresponded and differed. She was like him and yet different; no other part of creation corresponded like Eve. Unlike Grenz's understanding, Eve was not a savior, a term in theological circles applying only to Christ, but rather, a helper. The sexual differences were essential; they were important. Marriage, therefore, fulfills both purposes of sexuality, to unite and to generate. Without the female being both like him and unlike him, the dual purpose cannot be met. God could have chosen to propagate by any means other than sex, but he did not. Thus, sexual difference is essential.[28] Homosexuality cannot fulfill the two purposes of sexuality, nor can it appropriately account for the sexual differences with which God created humanity. Clearly, God designed covenant marriage to be heterosexual.

God Designed Covenant Marriage to be Fruitful

Thus far, one recognizes the moral restrictions of covenant marriage issue from being made male and female for a one flesh union. Two primary purposes for marriage arise from being made with sexual differences: to bond and to reproduce. God made them "male and female" and "the two shall become one;" hence, marriage is exclusive. In addition, God commands them "Be fruitful and multiply; fill the earth and subdue it; have dominion over the fish of the sea, over the birds of the air, and over every living thing that moves on the earth" (Gen 1:28). Thus, in one sense, God made them male and female in order that they might unite in a one flesh union of covenant marriage and fulfill his mandate to multiply. Covenant marriage establishes the parameters for procreation.

The fruitfulness of marriage has two dimensions: physical and spiritual. Clearly, God intended couples to physically multiply and bear children. The offspring of physical intimacy, moreover, Scripture calls a reward, "the fruit of the womb" (Ps 127: 3–4). The biblical record nowhere suggests couples will marry and not have children. To the contrary, the Bible consistently considers parenthood a blessing: "Blessed is the man whose quiver is full" (Ps 127:4). Psalm 128 contends the man who fears the Lord will be blessed, with the result that his wife will bear much fruit and his table will be surrounded with children (Ps 128:1–5). Hence, Scripture indicates God intended couples in marriage to be fruitful physically.[29]

Not only does Scripture intend for partners in marriage to reproduce, and thus have children, but also to reproduce spiritual children. For Luther, having children is the "chief purpose of marriage."[30] Marriage not only allows couples to fulfill their marital obligation, but it also permits a couple to rear children for Godly service. Scripture expects Christians to do more than bear children, which even the ungodly do; the Christian couple must raise their children well. That is, marriage should also be spiritually fruitful.

In *The Estate of Marriage*, Luther argues that having offspring is the greatest good in marriage, "because to God there can be nothing dearer than the salvation of souls."[31] It is the parents' responsibility to bring their children to a knowledge of salvation. In Luther's view, fathers and mothers "are apostles, bishops, and priests to their children, for it is they who make them acquainted with the gospel."[32]

Andreas Kostenberger makes a similar argument in his forthcoming "Marriage and the Family."[33] Commenting on Paul's letter to the Ephesians, Kostenberger asserts "the marriage relationship must be seen within the compass of God's larger salvation-historical, eschatological purposes, that is, the bringing of 'all things in heaven and on earth together under one head, even Christ' (1:10)."[34] Kostenberger develops this observation in his discussion of verse thirty-one: "and the two shall become one flesh." He writes:

> Paul's major point seems to be that marriage has the honor of embodying the "one-flesh" principle that later in salvation history became true spiritually also for the union of the exalted Christ with the church, which is described by Paul in terms of "head," "members," and "body." This, too, like the inclusion of Gentiles in God's salvific plan, is a *mysterion*: it was hidden in the divine wisdom in ages past but now has been given to Paul to reveal. Marriage is thus shown to be part and parcel of God's overarching salvation-historical purposes of "bringing all things together under one head, even Christ" (1:10). The lesson to be drawn from this is that marriage in Christian teaching, rather than being the be all and end all of human relationships, is to be subsumed under Christ's rule. Just as Christ must rule over all heavenly powers (1:21–22) and over the church (4:15), he must also rule over the marital relationship (5:21–33), the home (6:1–4), and the workplace (6:5–9). A married couple is part of the church (understood as family of families), and it too, is part of that spiritual warfare that resolutely resists evil (6:10–14) and seeks to promote God's purposes in this world (foremost the preaching of the gospel, 6:15–20).[35]

Thus, God's design for marriage includes promoting his purposes in the world, principally in bringing those spiritually lost to a relationship with the living Lord.

God intends marriage, therefore, to be the place for procreation. By issuing the command to multiply before the fall, moreover, God suggests that it is pure and good; no essential relationship exists between sex and sinfulness. Lastly, one cannot separate the command to procreate from the responsibility of parents to raise their children in the Lord and to witness to a fallen world.

God Designed Covenant Marriage to be Life-Long

In addition to God designing marriage to be an exclusive and fruitful, heterosexual relationship, God intends marriage to last for life. Earlier discussions showed that when God establishes a covenant marriage relationship, it is permanent: "Has the Lord not made them one" (Mal 2:15; see also Ezek 16:60)? The question in Malachi 2:15 means that because God establishes marriage as a lasting covenant, it must therefore be indissoluble. Christ himself stated, "Therefore what God has joined together, let not man separate" (Matt 19:6). Although numerous debates continue to surround the subject of divorce in Scripture, almost all commentators agree divorce was not intended from the beginning.[36] Paul articulates the idea this way: "For the woman who has a husband is bound by the law to her husband as long as he lives. But if the husband dies, she is released from the law of her husband" (Rom 7:2). Thus, marriage was intended to be life-long.[37]

Refusing to allow himself to be caught in the Pharisees' trap, Jesus enunciated God's intentions for marriage. First, Jesus recalled God made the first couple male and female. Second, God joined them together. Lastly, since God joined them, no human should attempt separation.[38] In other words, divorce would have been unimaginable "in the beginning." On the contrary, the two were to "become one." Thus, Moses may have permitted severing of the marital bond because of the hardness of one's heart, but it was not part of the order of creation. To the contrary, because God establishes the covenant and not the marriage partners, the relationship is inviolable.

Not only does God establish covenant marriage, but recall, God also serves as the enforcing authority (see Gen 31:50; Mal 2:15; and Pro 2:18). Calvin, for example, views God as a third party member to all marriages, acting as guarantor of the institution. In his commentary on Malachi he contends:

> [W]hen a marriage takes place between a man and a woman, God presides and requires a mutual pledge from both. Hence Solomon, in Proverbs ii.17, calls marriage the covenant of God, for it is superior to all human contracts. So also Malachi declares, that God is as it were the stipulator, who by his authority joins the man to the woman, and sanctions the alliance.[39]

Because marriage is a covenant, God fixes and enforces its norms, not man. Whereas human courts serve as the enforcing authority for human contracts, God alone sustains covenant marriage.

Third, because God sets the terms of marriage and not man, marital responsibilities are independent of the other party's behavior and thus, obligations in marriage are moral and unconditional. For example, even after the terms and obligations of the marriage covenant were broken, Malachi insisted "the wife of your youth" was still "the wife of your marriage covenant" (Mal 2:14–15). Similarly, God remained bound by his covenant with Israel though she played the harlot (Ezek 16:60). The unwavering testimony of Scripture points toward the life-long nature of a covenant relationship. Marriage lasts until the covenanters are parted by death.

Fourth, because marriage is a covenant, each member pledges his life and service. Malachi warned those considering breaking the bonds of marriage, "Take heed of your life" (Mal 2:16). The implication was clear: covenant marriage ought not be dissolved. Hence, most couples pledge during the marriage ceremony to be faithful "until parted by death."

Last, because the primary obligation in covenant marriage is love, divorce, by definition, violates it. That is, any attempt to separate from and abandon one's marriage partner cannot reflect marital love. Covenant love seeks what is best for the other. In *Basic Christian Ethics*, Paul Ramsey beautifully illustrates the enduring nature of covenant marriage:

> Adultery as the primary reason for divorce appears to be the natural and just order of human relationships when claims, what is "due," are being considered. . . . [A]nd everywhere, whatever the form of marriage, as long as marriage endures as an institution, there has been some definition of the faithfulness due one's partner in marriage, the legitimate claim of one, the acknowledged duty of the other partner. Thus, in the order of human claims, adultery, or failure to fulfill basic claims, comes first as reason for releasing the injured or innocent party from any further obligation within the marriage. Something like this line of reasoning both should and will find acceptance as long as the normal procedure for estimating rightful claims, and weighing refusal of what is due in terms of these claims, continues to be the primary consideration for preserving a marriage or bringing it to an end. For Jesus the order of claims upon another has been supplanted by a sequence dictated by another's needs: for this reason unchastity was for him not so decisive as nature and society teach us it is in the order of claims; and for him a marriage terminated for this as well as for any other reason represented some degree of failure to achieve God's purpose. Unclaiming love will hardly find any cause for divorce, least of all will it fasten first upon what is the chief reason for divorce in the attitude of a person mainly concerned to claim his own rights.[40]

Ramsey accurately asserts that divorce occurs primarily from the perceived violation of one or both marital members' 'rights'—one has not received what is due. This manner of reasoning typifies the process for most individuals. For Jesus, however, the primary concern was not receiving one's just claim, but rather, meeting the needs of the other partner. The obligation of covenant love focuses on the other and not self. Consequently, unchastity, though deplorable and hurtful, ceases to be a valid reason for divorce. Covenant love, to use Ramsey's words, "will hardly find any cause for divorce, least of all . . . in the attitude of a person mainly concerned to claim his own rights."

Theologians have long debated the indissolubility of the marriage bond (*vinculum conjugale*). The permanence of marriage, Aristotle contended, is unalterable: "*monou gar autou kai theos sterisketai, ageneta poiein ass' an e pepragmena.*"[41] Similarly, Thomas Aquinas wrote "*Deus non potest facere quod praeteritum non fuerit.*"[42] Philosophically, the *vinculum* may be understood as moral or ontological. For example, E. Schillebeeckx said in the patristic period marriage was seen as a "life commitment" that *ought* not to be dissolved, but in the medieval period marriage was an ontological bond that *could* not be broken. "These two visions—the patristic view of marriage as a moral obligation and the scholastic view of marriage as an ontological bond—are not mutually exclusive, but rather mutually implicit. Both the patristic and the scholastic doctrines are firmly based on Scripture."[43] Whether or not the bond is moral, ontological, or both, the question remains: Can the marriage bond be broken?[44] Theologians have long argued for the indissolubility of marriage on various grounds, including the nature of human sexuality and unalterability of the past.[45] Thus far I have argued for the life-long nature of marriage based upon its covenantal nature. That is, because God establishes covenant marriage and serves as its enforcing authority, he guarantees the marriage bond for life. Consequently, the marriage bond cannot be broken. Consider the following syllogism:

> *Marriage is a covenant;*
> *Covenants are indissoluble;*
> *Marriage is indissoluble.*

In light of the covenant argument for the indissolubility of marriage, how should one understand the divorce provision in the Mosaic Law (Deut 24:1–4) and the "exception clauses" in Matthew (5:31–32 and 19:8–9)? In the following discussion, I do not seek to revisit *in toto* the countless positions in the divorce and remarriage debate, but rather, I intend to offer some possible readings of Deuteronomy and Matthew that support the indissolubility of covenantal marriage advocated in this study.[46]

Arguments for the Indissolubility of Marriage in Deuteronomy

Any discussion concerning the indissolubility of marriage must deal with the divorce provision in the Mosaic Law (Deut 24:1–4). Can one simultaneously hold that the marriage bond cannot be broken and affirm the truth of Deuteronomy 24: "He writes her a certificate of divorce, puts it in her hand, and sends her out of his house" (Deut 24:1)? Although countless interpretations of this passage have been put forth, at least two interpretations of Deuteronomy weigh in favor of the indissolubility of the marriage bond, and are thus consistent with a covenantal reading: the kinship argument and the betrothal argument.

Kinship Argument

The majority of commentators interpreted the purpose of the divorce provision as a means for discouraging hasty divorce or for regarding second marriages as adulterous. In his article "The Restoration of Marriage," R. Yaron rejects the traditional explanations. With regard to the hasty divorce explanation, he writes, "If this had indeed been the purpose of the biblical law-giver [to stop a hasty divorce], the means he employed were curiously ineffective ones. When divorcing his wife a husband is not likely to take into account the legal situation which will arise after the dissolution of the subsequent marriage of his wife."[47] Because what the husband most wants is to be freed from his wife, he is not likely to consider a law forbidding him to remarry her.

With regard to explanations that stress second marriages are adulterous, Yaron writes that the Law does not address this issue. Rather, the restoration of the first marriage is prohibited. Yaron insists Deuteronomy twenty-four should be explained "by reference to another sphere, namely that of incest."[48] By outlawing remarriage to the first husband, the law protects the wife from possible tensions with her first husband who may seek to return to his wife. Thus, Yaron contends Deuteronomy twenty-four not only does not object to a second marriage, but "it takes effective steps to ensure its stability and continuation."[49]

Recently, Gordon Wenham responded to Yaron's explanation of Deuteronomy. Noting that the Law forbids remarriage even if the second husband dies, Wenham asks, "Why protect the second marriage when death has ended it?"[50] Building on Yaron's work, nevertheless, Wenham cites three reasons why the first husband should not take back a former wife after the death of her second husband: "she has been defiled;" "it is an abomination before the Lord;" and it "brings sin in the land" (Deut 24:4). Wenham links the notions of defilement, abomination, and pollution in the land with similar occurrences in Leviticus eighteen and twenty connected with sexual offences: "It will be suggested that the motive clauses of *Lev.* 18 and 20, which explain the levitical incest rules, may also provide the clue to the deuteronomic law about the restoration of marriage."[51]

Leviticus eighteen and twenty outlaw marriage between consanguines to the first and second degree. Consequently, one is not permitted to marry his mother or his sister (Lev 18:8–10) or his aunt (Lev 18:12). Similarly, Scripture forbids marriage between affines. Hence, one also may not marry the wife of his father, uncle, son, or brother (Lev 18:14–16). Scripture forbids these unions because they represent close relatives: "their nakedness is your own nakedness" (Lev 18:10). Wenham paraphrases verse ten, 'A man may not marry his granddaughters, because they are his own flesh and blood.'"[52] Wenham concludes that marital intercourse makes a man and his wife as closely related as parents and children. "Marriage thus creates both vertical blood-relationships in the form of children and horizontal 'blood'-relationships between spouses."[53]

Because marriage establishes a new and lasting relationship between marriage partners and their families, Wenham concludes Deuteronomy twenty-four forbids a divorced woman from remarrying her first husband. It would be as wrong as a man marrying his sister, which is described as "an abomination before the Lord" (Deut 24; and Jer 3:1). Whereas Yaron compared the general purpose of the Mosaic Law to incest rules, maintaining that it served to reduce tension between family circles, Wenham argued Deuteronomy actually regarded the restoration of marriage as incest.

Wenham's kinship argument is consistent with the covenant understanding of marriage in several ways. First, the kinship argument rests on the idea that marriage creates a new family unit. In chapter three we argued the author of Genesis implies biblical marriage involves the establishment of a new family unit between unrelated persons when he records a man must "leave" and "cleave" and they become "one flesh." Accordingly, Cassuto writes, "To leave and cleave simply means that when a man takes a wife, he creates a new family. So long as he is in his father's house, all his love is dedicated to his father and mother, but when he marries, his love for his wife transcends that for his parents."[54] Leaving denotes the establishment of a new family unit, and cleaving points to the committed faithfulness that one promises to the other; "that whatever the future holds, the couple intend to face it as a pair."[55] Like the covenantal view, therefore, the kinship argument includes the element of a new relationship that reaches beyond present blood ties. Second, the kinship argument affirms the permanent nature of the marriage bond. Marriage creates a kinship that even divorce could not break, effectively recognizing the indissolubility of the marriage bond.

Betrothal Argument

The betrothal argument represents a second argument from Deuteronomy consistent with the covenantal view of marriage. The heart of the betrothal argument rests on two key truths: the importance of a man not having sexual relations with his wife after she has had sex with another man and the importance of a bride's virginity.[56]

The story of David isolating the ten concubines with whom his son Absalom had had sexual intercourse illustrates the first truth: "So they were shut up to the day of their death, living in widowhood" (2 Sam 20:3; see also 2 Sam 16:20–21 and Gen 49:4). Describing the background for the law, Isaksson writes:

> If her intercourse with the other man took place before the consummation of the marriage, she was to be stoned to death (Deut 22:21) and the same was the case if it took place after the consummation of the marriage (Deut 22:22). Even when the intercourse took place after divorce (Deut 24:1–4) or under duress (2 Sam 16:21–22, 20:3), the wife became so unclean that further sexual cohabitation with her was inconceivable.[57]

The significance of not having sexual relations with a woman who had been with another man is reflected in the set of laws related to the second key truth: a bride's virginity. If at the marriage a bride was found not to be a virgin, she was to be stoned to death (Deut 22:21). If the husband falsely accused his wife of not having been a virgin, the elders of the city would fine him one hundred shekels of silver and he could not divorce her (Deut 22:18–19). Lastly, Scripture records that if a man and a betrothed virgin had sexual relations, both were to be put to death (Deut 22:23–27). Based on the importance of a bride's virginity, Isaksson concludes sexual intercourse is the decisive act consummating a marriage. The marriage was not completed until consummated in sexual intercourse.[58]

How do these two truths affect the interpretation of Deuteronomy twenty-four? The first pillar—that a man is not to have sexual relations with a woman after she has had sexual intercourse with another man—provides the foundation for why the reunion of a couple is forbidden even if the second husband dies. Once the divorced woman has been with another man, the first husband cannot take her back (Deut 24:4).

The second pillar—the importance of a bride's virginity—likewise, provides the foundation for understanding the justification given for the

Mosaic divorce: "and it happens that she finds no favor in his eyes because he has found some uncleanness [עֶרְוַת דָּבָר] in her" (Deut 24:1). Based upon the preceding discussion concerning the importance of a bride's virginity, the 'uncleanness' [עֶרְוַת דָּבָר] cannot be adultery or fornication.[59] It is highly doubtful that the author would prescribe death and divorce for fornication and adultery within the scope of twenty-five verses. To the contrary, the law was clear regarding the consequences for sexual infidelity: death. Whatever the nature of the 'uncleanness' [עֶרְוַת דָּבָר], it cannot include adultery or fornication. Consequently, this has led numerous theologians to conclude the betrothal period is the proper context in which Deuteronomy twenty-four must be understood.[60]

Betrothal was a legal contract for future marriage entered by either the parties themselves or their relatives.[61] More than a mere promise to marry, betrothal was the first stage of marriage, with the betrothed parties called 'husband' and 'wife' (Gen 29:21; Deut 22:23; Matt 1:18–25). Indeed, the couple was regarded in most respects as married, "though not yet entitled to the marital right nor bound to fulfill any of the mutual duties of conjugal life, as long as the marriage was not consummated by the nuptials."[62] Usually, an interval of about a year elapsed between the time of betrothal and the nuptials, primarily allowing time for the bride to make her outfit. "During this period she lived with her friends, and every intimate intercourse between herself and her future husband was strictly prohibited."[63] Lastly, the betrothment could be dissolved only by means of death or a formal bill of divorce, which could be granted only because of some faithlessness on the part of the female. Therefore, according to the betrothal argument, Deuteronomy twenty-four allows for the dissolution of a betrothed couple, as long as the relationship had not been consummated. Once the couple had engaged in sexual intercourse, a different set of laws applied (Deut 22). Hence, the betrothal argument contains several factors that are consistent with the covenant view of marriage.

First, the betrothal view recognizes the indissoluble nature of the marriage bond once the relationship has been consummated. Scripture prescribes specific measures after the discovery of sexual infidelity, actions that are incompatible with the bill of divorcement permitted in Deuteronomy twenty-four. Allowing the dissolution of a consummated marriage for any 'uncleanness' trivializes marriage in a manner inconsistent with the high view of marriage.

Second, the betrothal view fits well with the high view of marriage God obviously desires. Only the dissolution of a betrothed marriage comports to the moral repugnance against the possibility of remarriage that is expressed in Scripture: "an abomination before the Lord" (Deut 24:4; see also Jer 3:1). Consistent with the covenant view, proponents of the betrothal argument maintain marriage is life-long. Therefore, the kinship and betrothal arguments in Deuteronomy both support the covenantal view that marriage is life-long and cannot be broken. Now we turn our attention to addressing the "exception clauses" in the gospel of Matthew.

Arguments Supporting the Indissolubility of Marriage in Matthew

The second hurdle that must be overcome by proponents of the covenant view of marriage is how to interpret the "exception clauses" in the first gospel. Matthew writes:

> Furthermore it has been said, "Whoever divorces his wife, let him give her a certificate of divorce." But I say to you that whoever divorces his wife for any reason except sexual immorality [παρεκτὸς λόγου πορνείας] causes her to commit adultery; and whoever marries a woman who is divorced commits adultery (Matt 5:31–32).

> Moses, because of the hardness of your hearts, permitted you to divorce your wives, but from the beginning it was not so. And I say to you, whoever divorces his wife, except for sexual immorality [μὴ ἐπὶ πορνείᾳ], and marries another, commits adultery; and whoever marries her who is divorced commits adultery (Matt 19:8–9).

At least five interpretations of the Matthean passages support the covenantal view that marriage is life-long and thus, human parties are unable to sever the marriage bond. Each of these arguments hinge on the interpretation of two phrases: παρεκτὸς λόγου πορνείας and μὴ ἐπὶ πορνείᾳ.[64]

Inclusivist Argument

The first rationale for handling the Matthean "exception clauses" while simultaneously holding to the life-long nature of the marriage bond is the inclusivist argument. According to this view, the phrase μὴ ἐπὶ πορνείᾳ should be translated "not even in the case of uncleanness."[65] Brunec contends ἐπὶ means "over and above", "outside (the case)," and μὴ means "even not." Thus, he explains the exception denotes "even not outside the case of uncleanness"—"even inclusive of the case of uncleanness" (Matt 19:9). Brunec makes a similar argument with Matthew 5:32. Hence, the proponents of the inclusivist argument contend Jesus permits no ground for divorce, "even in the case of adultery," and as a result, support the life-long nature of marriage. Although the inclusivist argument for the "exception clauses" can be used to support the covenant view that marriage is indissoluble, it has a weakness.

Brunec seems to argue from exceptions in the Greek to absolutes. That is, sometimes a context may require the reader mentally to supply a word. However, Vawter notes, "It is simply begging the question to supply the word wherever [one desires] then, on the basis of the supplement, conclude to the type of proposition which alone makes it possible."[66] Therefore, it is doubtful the inclusivist argument represents the most faithful interpretation of the text.

Preteritive Argument

Bruce Vawter presents a second argument for handling the Matthean "exceptions." According to preteritive argument the exception clauses are preteritions—they are exceptions to the proposition itself. First, Vawter discusses the meaning of three key words: παρεκτὸς, μὴ, and ἐπὶ. First, παρεκτὸς means "outside," "without," or "apart from" and governs the phrase λόγου πορνείας. Hence, Vawter contends the exception is not to the prohibition of dismissing a wife, but to the consideration itself. Second, μὴ nullifies the force of the preposition ἐπὶ. Third, ἐπὶ, whose basal meaning is of position, 'upon,' logically has the force of signifying circumstance or state when employed with an abstract noun. μὴ ἐπὶ πορνείᾳ is a negative adverbial phrase which modifies, again, not the verb "dismiss" but the Lord's entire assertion." Thus, Vawter punctuates Matthew:

> I say to you, however, that everyone who dismisses his wife—setting aside the matter or porneia [παρεκτὸς λόγου πορνείᾳ]—makes her become an adulteress; and whoever marries her who has been dismissed, commits adultery (Matt 5:32).
>
> I say to you, however that if anyone dismisses his wife—porneia is not involved [μὴ ἐπὶ πορνείᾳ]—and marries another, he commits adultery; and whoever marries one who has been dismissed, commits adultery (Matt 19:9).[67]

The Lord, therefore, refused to comment on the issue of πορνείᾳ. Why then did Jesus bring up the case of πορνείᾳ? Proponents for the preteritive view aver that the Pharisees were asking Jesus to interpret the Mosaic law on divorce (Deut 24:1–4). Their question centered on the law's meaning of "uncleanness" [עֶרְוַת דָּבָר]. Does it mean "adultery" or can it mean "any reason whatever" (Matt 19:9)? Thus, the Pharisees were not questioning the legality of divorce, a fact they assumed, but rather, the proper grounds for the divorce.

According to the preteritive view, Jesus did not answer this question—the legal grounds for divorce. Rather, he asserted the absolute indissolubility of marriage based on the order of creation. Shocked by his answer, the Pharisees asked *why* the Mosaic provision for divorce. Jesus responded that Moses' concession was an "interim legislation in the true sense, contrary to the ideal of the Law and to the antecedent will of God."[68] Therefore, Jesus did not answer their question regarding the grounds for divorce nor did he condone the provisions for it. And so he concludes, "I say to you, whoever dismisses his wife—Deut 24:1 notwithstanding—and marries another, commits adultery."[69]

Positively, the preteritive argument allows for the life-long nature of the marriage bond, consistent with the covenant view of marriage. Negatively, however, it reflects a low view of Scripture. That is, the preteritive view denies the internal consistency of God's Word, supposing the Old Testament condones divorce and the New Testament does not. Hence, the preteritive argument, while supporting the covenant view, does not represent the best option for evangelicals.

Mixed Marriage Argument

A third option for handling the Matthean exceptions and affirming the life-long nature of marriage is the mixed marriage argument. According to this argument, πορνεία refers to marriages between Jews and Gentiles. Because the law forbade Jews from intermarrying (Deut 7:3), and because Ezra commanded the covenant men to divorce heathen women (Ezra 9–10), and because Matthew is written to a predominantly Jewish audience, supporters of this view maintain Jesus is allowing the dissolution of interfaith marriages. Just as Ezra sought to keep the Jewish line pure and free from idolatry, some proponents of this view insist Jesus permitted divorce for the preservation of the Jewish people and their faith.[70] Other supporters contend Jesus legitimized the divorce only for the case explained in Ezra.[71]

Although mixed marriage argument is consistent with a high view of marriage affirmed by Scripture, it still has some weaknesses. If mixed marriages represent the only reason for divorce in the New Testament, it remains unclear why Joseph is considered a righteous man for intending to divorce Mary for reasons other than different faiths (Matt 1:18–25). Moreover, for πορνείᾳ to have such a limited understanding appears to be a stretch of the language.

Kinship Argument

A fourth option for handling the Matthean exceptions and affirming the life-long nature of marriage is the kinship argument.[72] Supporters of this view claim πορνείᾳ in Matthew chapters five and nineteen is equivalent to the Hebrew *zenuṯ*, which refers to illegitimate marriages within the bounds of consanguinity and affinity found in Leviticus 18:6–8. F. F. Bruce contends this interpretation is consistent with the use of πορνείᾳ in Acts 15:20–29: "The prohibition of fornication [πορνείᾳ] understood generally, is of course an ethical prohibition in both forms of the text, but the word may be used here in a more specialized sense, of marriage within degrees of blood-relationship or affinity forbidden by the legislation of Lev. 18:52."[73] Fitzmyer makes the same observation based upon the similarity of prohibitions found in the Holiness Code (Lev 17–18) and Jerusalem Decree (Acts 15:22–29):

> The letter of James to the local churches of Antioch, Syria, an Cilicia forbids, in fact, four of the things proscribed by the Holiness Code of Lv 17–18, not only for 'a man of the house of Israel' but also for 'strangers that sojourn among them' . . . These were the meat offered to idols (Lv 17:8–0), the eating of blood (Lv 17:10–12), the eating of strangled, i.e., not properly butchered animals (Lv 17:15; cf Ex 22:31), and intercourse with close kin (Lv 18:6–18).[74]

The Apostle Paul makes a similar link between incest and πορνείᾳ: "It is actually reported *that there is* sexual immorality [πορνείᾳ] among you, and such sexual immorality [πορνείᾳ] as is not even named among the Gentiles—that a man has his father's wife" (1 Cor 5:1)! In this context, Paul clearly equates "sexual immorality" with incest. Based upon the technical understanding of πορνείᾳ, therefore, proponents of the kinship view argue Jesus allows for the annulment of incestuous marriages. Far from giving a general justification for divorce, Jesus restates that incestuous marriages are forbidden.

Like the previous arguments presented in this section, the kinship argument recognizes the life-long nature of marriage by rejecting the claim that Jesus gave a general justification for divorce. Second, by equating πορνείᾳ with the forbidden marriages in Leviticus, proponents of this view are able to link the kinship arguments of Deuteronomy and Matthew. As a result, this view recognizes the internal consistency between the Old and New Testaments. Negatively, however, if the kinship view is correct and Jesus allows separation based only on incestuous relationships, it is difficult to explain how Scripture can call Joseph a "righteous man" when he sought to "put away" Mary for supposed adultery, a reason not permitted by Jesus if the kinship view is correct. That is, why does Matthew call Joseph a "righteous man" for attempting to do what Christ did not allow? Because the kinship argument appears unable to answer this question, another option is more likely, despite the kinship argument weighing in favor of a covenantal understanding of the marriage bond.

Betrothal Argument[75]

The fifth option for handling the Matthean exceptions and affirming the life-long nature of marriage is the betrothal argument. The foundation for this view is two-fold: recognizing the Old Testament law allowed no provisions for breaking the marriage covenant once the relationship had been consummated by sexual intercourse; and recognizing the audience to whom Matthew was writing.

First, proponents of this view assume that Deuteronomy twenty-four deals with a betrothal and not a sexually consummated marriage. Thus, the Mosaic law is not a general provision for divorce but an exception for allowing the dissolution of a promise to marry based upon the discovery of some dishonesty.[76] Second, supporters of this view stress the importance of Matthew's Jewish audience. Isaksson emphasizes that the "exception clauses" are not present in the Lukan and Markan parallels (Mark 10:11–12 and Luke 16:8). That is, to the Gentile audiences, Jesus clearly denied any grounds for divorce: "Whoever divorces his wife and marries another commits adultery against her. And if a woman divorces her husband and marries another, she commits adultery" (Mark 10:11–12). Thus, proponents of the betrothal argument conclude, Matthew's inclusion of the "exception clauses" must be related to the Jewishness of his audience, for example, the betrothal.

Theologians subscribing to the betrothal argument insist the Pharisees questions were designed to trap Jesus in the Jewish controversy concerning the proper grounds for a divorce. The two main schools of thought, Shammai and Hillel, interpreted the phrase דָּ'בָר' עֶרְוַת differently. The school of Shammai interpreted the law strictly, teaching that a wife should not be divorced except for unfaithfulness. The *Mishnah* reads, "Beth Shammai say: a man should not divorce his wife unless he has found her guilty of some unseemly conduct, as it says, because he hath found some unseemly thing in her."[77] Thus, the school of Shammai based its interpretation of Deuteronomy on the word עֶרְוַת. The school of Hillel, however, interpreted the phrase more liberally, seizing on the word 'דְּבַר'. Consequently, the school of Hillel permitted divorce for practically any reason (see Matt 19:3). "Beth Hillel, however, say [that he may divorce her] even if she has merely spoilt his food . . . even if he finds another woman more beautiful than she is."[78] Thus, the Pharisees put Jesus in a position of having to choose a particular school of thought, a choice that was bound to incense one group.

Rather than commit to either position regarding the grounds for divorce, Jesus challenged the basis of their question; Jesus objected to any justification of divorce. Instead of discussing Deuteronomy, Jesus quoted Genesis, where God established and defined his intentions for marriage: "Have you not read that 'he who made them at the beginning made them male and female' and said, 'for this reason a man shall leave his father and mother and be joined to his wife, and the two shall become one flesh" (Matt 19:4–5). Jesus insisted that marriage is not a mere social institution to be governed by human laws, but rather, it is a divine covenant subject to and governed by the laws of God.[79]

Having challenged the basis of their original question, the Pharisees asked Jesus, "Why then did Moses command to give a certificate of divorce, and to put her away" (Matt 19:7)? Jesus responded: "And I say to you, whoever divorces his wife, except for sexual immorality [μὴ ἐπὶ πορνείᾳ], and marries another, commits adultery; and whoever marries her who is divorced commits adultery" (Matt 19:9). The only way that a second marriage could be adulterous is if the first marriage continues to exist. Thus, marriage is indissoluble.

How then should one handle the "exception clauses"? Proponents of the betrothal argument contend the word πορνείᾳ refers to premarital unchastity during the Jewish betrothal period.[80] By the time of Christ, two options were available to a husband who discovered his wife had not maintained her chastity before marriage: he might present his case to the city judges and have her put to death (Deut 22:20–21); or he might write her a "bill of divorce" (Deut 24:1).[81] The story of Joseph and Mary illustrate the second option:

> After his mother Mary was betrothed to Joseph, before they came together, she was found with child of the Holy Spirit. Then Joseph her husband, being a just man, and not wanting to make her a public example, was minded to put her away secretly (Matt 1:18–19).

As Matthew presents the story, Joseph had reason to believe Mary had been sexually unfaithful while they were betrothed. Not desiring to "make her a public example," and thus have her stoned, he chose to write her a bill of divorce and "put her away secretly." Later, having been informed by an angel of the Lord that the child in Mary was conceived by the Holy Spirit, Joseph did as the Lord commanded him and took Mary to be his wife (Matt 1:20–25). The word πορνεία, therefore, should be understood as referring to the same kind of unchastity as that Joseph suspected Mary—premarital unchastity.

Understood in this manner, Jesus' "exception" for πορνεία affirms the indissoluble nature of the marriage bond. Far from giving a general justification for breaking the marriage covenant, Jesus permitted "divorce" only for marriages which had not yet been consummated by sexual intercourse. In contemporary jargon, Jesus merely allowed for the dissolution of a promise to marry. Jesus used the term 'divorce' in the original betrothal sense.[82]

Christ, therefore, completely rejected the Pharisaic interpretation of Deuteronomy twenty-four and refused to affirm either the Shammai or Hillel options. Instead, Christ appealed to God's original intentions by which a couple is joined together in an inseparable one flesh union for life. The only justification for divorce allowed by Christ was the termination of a betrothal marriage prior to consummation of the marriage relationship by sexual intercourse. Surprised by Jesus' interpretation of the Mosaic law, the disciples said, "If such is the case [that a man cannot divorce his wife after she has proven to be immoral and unfaithful], it is better not to marry" (Matt 19:10). The reaction of the disciples would not make sense if Jesus supported one of the prevailing schools of thought.[83]

The betrothal argument is consistent with the covenantal view of marriage. First, it affirms the life-long nature of the marriage bond. The betrothal argument allows for no divorce once a marriage is consummated by sexual intercourse. Second, the betrothal argument affirms the internal consistency of the Old and New Testaments. Jesus' teaching in Matthew does not contradict the Mosaic law. Third, the betrothal view affirms a high view of marriage God obviously desires. The betrothal view explains God's moral revulsion regarding the possibility of divorce and remarriage in Jeremiah (Jer 3:1) and Deuteronomy (Deut 24:4) and the exception clauses in Matthew's gospel. Therefore, several arguments from Deuteronomy and from Matthew weigh in favor of the covenantal view that marriage is life-long.

In summary, God establishes and upholds covenant marriage. Moreover, because God fixed the terms of covenant marriage at creation, marital responsibilities are independent of another's behavior; obligations are moral and unconditional. Love, therefore, as the pre-eminent covenant obligation, is a moral duty, one that seeks to meet the other's needs and not one's own. Accordingly, divorce violates the responsibility of love and the scriptural intention of biblical marriage, which God designed to be life-long.[84]

God Designed Covenant Marriage to be Ordered

Thus far, God having designed marriage to be a covenant implies the husband-wife relationship is exclusive, heterosexual, fruitful, and life-long. In addition to these moral ramifications, God also designed marriage to be ordered, which means each party has certain defined responsibilities fixed by God at creation.

It has already been established that covenants have obligations. McCarthy writes, for example:

> All covenants . . . have their conditions. They must be defined somehow or other. These definitions are their conditions or stipulations which may often be assumed, things which are simply so well known in a culture that they need not be stated explicitly.[85]

Hence, some covenant obligations may be culturally conditioned, but exist nonetheless.

The study not only maintains covenant marriage by definition entails certain duties, but furthermore, covenant marriage places the greater responsibility on the husband. Hugenberger argues, moreover, that these obligations are evident from the mode of creation.[86] Nevertheless, covenant marriage still makes certain demands on the wife; she is a "helper comparable to him [עֵזֶר כְּנֶגְדּוֹ]" (Gen 2:18).[87]

Not all theologians recognize and accept the validity of God-ordained roles for men and women. Consider, for example, the recent publication, *Marriage Made in Eden*, by Alice Mathews and Gay Hubbard—professor and guest lecturer at Gordon-Conwell Seminary respectively. In it, they explore God's design and purpose for marriage. Mathews and Hubbard claim that the purpose of the book is to explore "what God had in mind when he designed marriage and how the purpose of marriage is both to transform us and to witness to God's grace and power in a sinful world." In order to accomplish this task, they seek to answer two questions: "First, what is marriage as a social institution in this present culture? Second, what does marriage *for God's people* look like in this present time, in this present culture?"[88]

Mathews and Hubbard develop their case for egalitarianism by examining specific passages in the canon. First, they discuss passages from Genesis, which they affirm describes what God had in mind when he designed humans and marriage. The Genesis narrative expresses the foundation of God's design for marriage: "For this reason a man will leave his father and mother and be united to his wife, and they will become one flesh" (Gen. 2:24). The phrase, "for this reason," reflects God's relational imperative that led to Eve's creation. "God did *not* say, 'Adam has too much work to do. Let's send help.' God did *not* say, 'Adam is the important First Man of humanity. Let's send someone to cook and clean for him.' God did *not* say, 'Adam needs help in making babies.' What God *did* say was, 'Adam is alone. That aloneness is not good. Let's make someone like him so that he will be alone no longer.'"[89]

Matthews and Hubbard continue their argument against God-ordained roles maintaining God gave his command to be fruitful and to subdue the earth to both men and women. "Both are to share in parenting, and both are to share in dominion."[90] The fall, they contend, introduced conflict into the marriage relationship. Consequently, Adam began to exert power over Eve, a pattern that was unknown in the Garden.[91] Mathew and Hubbard insist that marriage is not about a hierarchy of privilege, authority, or importance. "Marriage does not provide a job description detailing the assignment of the tasks of daily living."[92] Rather, marriage is about helping and caring for one another. God's desire to restore his creation to shared parenting and shared provision has not changed, and the present tension in marriage is being resolved by the coming of Jesus Christ.

Mathews and Hubbard also address various New Testament passages that speak of the husband being the head of his wife and of the wife being in submission to her husband. The authors insist that proper interpretation and application of Scripture necessarily involves determining which commands and practices were for only the audience to which they were given and which ones are permanent and binding for all people in all places at all times. Mathews and Hubbard note that the New Testament has six "household codes," three of which specifically address the husband/wife relationship: Ephesians 5:15–33; Colossians 3:18–19; and 1 Peter 3:1–9. The authors contend that Peter's passage, much like Paul's letters to Timothy and Titus, was based upon already existing hierarchical structures and was introduced to maintain order within society.[93] Their missional character is evidenced by Paul's statement "to give the enemy no opportunity for slander" (1 Tim. 5:14). When Peter writes that women are to submit to their own husbands, he is speaking of a voluntary act for the purpose of demonstrating the gospel, not because men have any God-ordained authority.

Similarly, Paul's injunction in Ephesians is not about authority, they claim. The phrase, "For the husband is head of the wife as Christ is head of the church" does not establish a doctrine of headship, which Mathews and Hubbard note is not a biblical term or biblical concept. They maintain that "head of his wife" is not defined in Scripture, but rather, it is described as a metaphor of two becoming one flesh. "Whatever else this metaphor carries, it is not linked to authority," assert Mathews and Hubbard.[94] Although they do not discuss Paul's passage of 1 Corinthians 11:3 in the text, they do make a similar argument in the endnotes. "Those who insist on interpreting *head* to mean 'leader' or 'ruler' or 'authority over' trip up on 1 Corinthians 11:3, which states that 'the head of Christ is God.' While there are other dangers in a doctrine of subordination in the Trinity, in its simplest form it ignores the three-in-oneness of the Godhead."[95] Hence, Mathews and Hubbard reject the notion that Scripture defines certain roles based upon gender. Specifically, the complementarian view cannot find support in the writings of Peter and Paul in the New Testament nor in a doctrine of subordination in the Godhead. They conclude, "Only one passage in the New Testament explicitly addresses the question of authority in marriage": 1 Corinthians 7:2–5. In this passage, Paul makes clear that authority in marriage relationships is *mutual* (211–12). Since our bodies belong to God, we can trust them to our mates.

With regard to Scripture, Mathews and Hubbard correctly write that God designed marriage and that proper interpretation of God's design requires readers to lay aside personal agendas. They are also right when they point to the creation narrative as the most important passages regarding male/female relationships because there God expresses the foundation of his design for marriage. However, I am convinced that their incomplete handling of these passages leads to a distorted view of God's intentions for men and women within the family and the church and contributed to their choice not to include discussions in the main text on such important passages as 1 Corinthians 11:3–16 and 1 Timothy 2:11–14. Since the creation narrative is most important to the discussion, it is difficult to imagine why Mathews and Hubbard would not discuss these two passages, especially since they appeal directly to Genesis. Perhaps, the exclusion of these passages in the text reveals the authors' failure to grasp or explain fully the centrality of the creation story for the present debate.

Mathews and Hubbard are correct that Genesis 1:26–28 teaches the equality of men and women, even presenting man and woman as co-rulers and equally necessary for multiplication. Thus, they correctly note that Scriptures proposes that participants in marriage share dominion and parenting. They incorrectly deduce, however, that shared dominion excludes God-ordained, gender-designed roles. Their confusion stems from a failure to comprehend fully chapter two of Genesis. There, Scripture says that God created man first (2:7–9), charged him to care for the garden (2:15–17), and provided him with a set of laws to enforce in the garden. God even commanded man to name the animals, as well as the woman (2:19–23). Hence, the male was the first one to care for the garden, to subdue it, and to enjoy dominion. Consequently, he bore ultimate responsibility before God for the initial mandate to subdue the earth and rule over it. In fact, he could have performed this task alone, but God said it was not good. Accordingly, God made man a helper, not in order that the garden have another leader, but rather, that man may have a helper, connoting functional responsibility. A proper understanding of the relationship between the sexes must include elements from both chapters: Genesis one and two. If this is done, one may rightly conclude that men and women are equal—they are both image bearers—and that they have different roles—the man is to lead and the woman is to come alongside and help.

The New Testament passages excluded from the book lend credence to this interpretation. For example, in his first letter to the church at Corinth, Paul taught that "the head of woman is man" because man was created first: "For man is not from woman, but woman from man" (11:8). Mathews and Hubbard incredibly avoid mentioning Paul's division of roles in his letter to Timothy. There Paul explicitly based his reasoning on the fact that "Adam was formed first, then Eve" (2:13). It is difficult to deny the importance of God creating men and women at different times and of creating man first. One has either to ignore New Testament passages which teach that this is important, or to re-interpret these passages by arguing Paul misunderstood the Old Testament, effectively calling into question the inspiration of Scripture. It is inadequate for Mathews and Hubbard to dismiss the topic of "headship" by merely stating "it is not a biblical term nor is it a biblical concept."[96] Rather, it is incumbent upon the authors to explain Paul's appeal to the creation narrative for his discussion of the gender roles. In light of this information, one struggles to comprehend Mathews and Hubbard's claim that 1 Corinthians 7:2–5 is the only New Testament passage that deals with the issue of authority in marriage.

Mathews and Hubbard do seek to address three of the passages which deal with the husband/wife relationship: Ephesians 5:15–33; Colossians 3:18–19; and 1 Peter 3:1–9. While they are right to note the missional character of these passages, they wrongly conclude, I believe, that these passages do not attend to the issue of authority within the marriage relationship.

In Ephesians, Paul discusses the husband-wife relationship with regard to the Christ-church relationship. For example, the husband-wife relationship described in 22–23a is supported by an exposition of the Christ-church relationship in verses 23b–24a. Likewise, the husband-wife relationship in 24b–25a is illumined by the relationship espoused by Christ and the church in 25b–27. Lastly, the two relationships are brought together in verses 31–32 by a direct quote from Genesis 2:24. Hence, the primary focus of Ephesians 5:21–33 is human marriage as it is illumined by the Christ-church relationship. Paul's appeal to the Genesis narrative directs the reader's attention to God's design at creation: equal natures with the man leading and the woman helping.

The context of Ephesians details the kind of submission that Paul has in mind: wives submit to their husbands (5:22–23), children submit to their parents (6:1–3), and slaves submit to their masters (6:5–8). The egalitarian claim that Paul insists on a "mutual submission" contradicts the context of Paul's argument and revises the church's historical understanding of this passage.[97] It would be absurd to suggest that Paul believes parents should submit to their children or masters to their slaves. Equally outrageous is the egalitarian claim for husbands to submit to their wives.[98] Interpreted consistently, Scripture asserts God-ordained roles for men and women. Not only does this appear to be the straightforward reading of Genesis, but it is also the New Testament's interpretation and application of the creation narrative. Scripture indicates God designed each with certain responsibilities—one leading and the other helping. Barth writes:

> At this point something must also be said about the question of the supremacy of the male and the subordination of the female in marriage. The question has been confused on both sides . . . What else can supremacy and subordination mean here but that the male is male and the female is female . . . The simple test is that when two people live together in demonstration of free mutual love this separation of functions will just take place . . . in all freedom . . . so that in fact the husband will precede and the wife follow.[99]

Barth insists within marriage, one will naturally lead and the other follow, accurately reflecting what it means to be male and female.

That God ordered marriage in this manner, with the husband accepting the role of leader and the wife of a helper, finds support in later Scripture. It is not accidental that a majority of passages dealing with the husband-wife relationship appeals to Genesis for proof of God's design. Later Scripture, such as Ephesians 5:21–33, 1 Timothy 2:8–15, 2 Corinthians 11:2–3, and 1 Peter 3:1–6, appeals to the Pentateuch for claims regarding the position of women in marriage. Clearly, God designed covenant marriage to be ordered.

Conclusion

Based upon the previous theological observations that issue from God designing marriage as a covenant relationship, one may recognize resulting moral implications. Consequently, having demonstrated its basis upon being made male and female, covenant marriage was shown to be heterosexual and fruitful, each reflecting the fundamental nature of sexual differences. Moreover, God made them male and female in order that they might become one, stressing the exclusivity and lasting character of covenant marriage. Lastly, it was shown that God established covenant marriage with certain obligations, with greater responsibility being given to the husband and the wife serving as a helper. That is, the husband and wife have God-ordained functions established before the fall. Hence, God designed covenant marriage to be ordered.

SUMMARY

I began this study by discussing three historical models for understanding marriage: sacramental, covenant, and contract. After examining the major models of marriage, the I sought to demonstrate the majority of society, including the church, seldom treat marriage as God designed it, which accounts for the general state of crisis currently surrounding the institution. Furthermore, this crisis in marriage largely corresponds to society's shift from viewing marriage as an institution designed by God to understanding marriage merely as an agreement between two individuals. Therefore, in order for the church to counter the current dilemma surrounding marriage, it is imperative to discover how God, at creation, designed marriage. Hence, the following four chapters proved the thesis that God, at creation, designed marriage to be a covenant relationship,

First, I defined what is meant by the term 'covenant.' Whereas scholars have historically approached defining it through diverse methods, such as the history of religions, philology, and theology, I outlined three reasons for adopting the biblical-concept definition proposed by Hugenberger. Biblical writers use covenant in a variety of situations, allowing it to be understood in different "senses." Understood in its primary Old Testament sense, I adopted the following definition of "covenant:" an elected, as opposed to natural, relationship of obligation established under divine sanction. As a result, four essential elements of a covenant were delineated: (1) personal relationship; (2) with a non-relative; (3) involving obligations; and (4) is established under oath. In addition to these essential elements, various general features were also noted. For instance, covenants were implied to be unilaterally dependent on the will and authority of God, resulting in morally-binding obligations. Compliance with these terms is relevant and may be tied to the reception of blessings and sanctions. Covenants are also characterized by a name change for the weaker partner, which signifies one stands under the authority and protection of another, and a sign that validates the covenant.

In order to demonstrate that God, at creation, designed marriage to be a covenant relationship, I explored the first two chapters of Genesis. Upon a detailed inspection of Genesis, I presented evidence that the paradigmatic relationship of Adam and Eve contained all the essential elements and general features of a covenant, suggesting marriage was created as a covenant relationship. Moreover, I insisted that Malachi considered marriage as a covenant and appealed to Genesis 2:24 as the basis for his claim, bolstering the assertion that God designed marriage as a covenant relationship in the beginning.

In chapter four I demonstrated subsequent passages in Scripture dealing with marriage support its covenantal nature as well. Hosea, Proverbs, and Ezekiel reinforce the idea of covenant marriage by metaphorically describing the covenant relationship between God and Israel as a marriage. In the New Testament, Ephesians, Matthew, and Mark inter-textually link their discussions of the husband-wife relationship to Old Testament passages identifying marriage as covenant. Most emphatically, Matthew and Mark's treatment of marriage parallel several Old Testament covenant passages by discussing marriage within the context of God's abhorrence for divorce and his original intentions for a "one flesh" union. Therefore, reasonable evidence was supplied for believing God, at creation, designed marriage to be a covenant relationship.

Having demonstrated the plausibility of marriage as a covenant relationship, chapter six summarized eight resulting theological observations: (1) God establishes covenant marriage; (2) marriage is fundamentally covenantal; (3) God enforces covenant marriage; (4) obligations in covenant marriage are moral; (5) obligations in covenant marriage are unconditional; (6) covenant marriage is secured by one's life and service; (7) covenant marriage finds its basis in what it means to be made male and female in the image of God for one flesh union; and (8) covenant marriage places greater responsibility on the husband. Consequently, I delineated five moral implications: (1) God designed marriage to be exclusive; (2) God designed covenant marriage to be heterosexual; (3) God designed covenant marriage to be fruitful; (4) God designed covenant marriage to be life-long; and (5) God designed covenant marriage to be ordered. In conclusion, marriage outside the beautiful parameters of covenantal love holds no value for either partner. Additionally, the blessings experienced through a covenanted bond ensure the Lord's hand upon his creation of a one flesh union between man and wife.

NOTES

1. Walter C. Kaiser Jr., *Toward Old Testament Ethics* (Grand Rapids: Zondervan Publishing Company, 1983), 31. For a discussion of the "orders of creation," see Carl F. H. Henry, *Christian Personal Ethics* (Grand Rapids: William B. Eerdmans Publishing Company, 1957), 242–6; John Murray, *Principles of Conduct: Aspects of Biblical Ethics*, 2d ed. (Grand Rapids: William B. Eerdmans Publishing Company, 1994), 27–81.

2. Ralph Elliott, *The Message of Genesis* (Nashville: Broadman Press, 1961), 170.

3. Gordon Paul Hugenberger, *Marriage As a Covenant: A Study of Biblical Law and Ethics Governing Marriage Developed From the Perspective of Malachi* (Leiden: E. J. Brill, 1994), 184.

4. See M. Weinfeld, "*Berith*" in *Theological Dictionary of the Old Testament*, ed. G. Johannes Botterweck, trans. John T. Willis (Grand Rapids: William B. Eerdmans Publishing Company, 1975), 2:225–79; Joseph A. Fitzmyer, "The Matthean Divorce Texts and Some New Palestinian Evidence," *Theological Studies* 37 (1976): 204; William A. Heth and Gordon J. Wenham, *Jesus and Divorce: The Problem with the Evangelical Consensus* (Nashville: Thomas Nelson Publishers, 1994), 103; and Paul Hoffman, "Jesus' Saying About Divorce and Its Interpretation in the New Testament Tradition," *Concillium* 55 (1970): 55–6.

5. See also Kaiser, *Toward Old Testament Ethics*, 139–243.

6. Karl Barth, *Church Dogmatics*, ed. G.W. Bromiley and T. F. Torrance (Edinburgh: T. & T. Clark, 1936–1969), 3.1.184.

7. See Dennis J. McCarthy, *Treaty and Covenant: A Study in Form in the Ancient Oriental Documents and in the Old Testament* (Rome: Biblical Institute, 1981), 106. In addition, McCarthy has an interesting discussion of familial analogies and covenants, though he incorrectly understands marriage at times to be a contract rather than a covenant: McCarthy, *Old Testament Covenant*, 33–4. For example see Am 1:9; 2 Sam 7:12–14 and Jer 31:9.

8. See Hugenberger, *Marriage as a Covenant*, 179. Compare Deut 6:5; 7:8, 13; 23:5; 30:6, 15, 16, 20.

9. See Hugenberger, *Marriage as Covenant*, 182.

10. See Gordon D. Fee, *The First Epistle to the Corinthians* (Grand Rapids: William B. Eerdmans Publishing Company, 1987), 266.

11. For a discussion of sexual union and its affect on a relationship, see Linda Woodhead, "Sex in a Wider Context," in *Sex These Days: Essays on Theology, Sexuality and Society*, ed. Jon Davies and Gerard Loughlin (Sheffield: Sheffield Academic Press, 1997), 111.

12. Compare the different list of sins mentioned in Hosea 2.

13. See Daniel Heimbach's discussion on self-stimulation in *True Sexual Morality: Recovering Biblical Standards for a Culture in Crisis* (Wheaton: Crossway Books, 2004), 222–223.

14. Martin Luther, "The Estate of Marriage (1522)", in *Luther's Works*, ed. Walther I. Brandt and Helmut T. Lehmann, trans. Walther I. Brandt (Philadelphia: Muhlenberg Press, 1962), 45:17.

15. Stanley J. Grenz, *Sexual Ethics: An Evangelical Perspective*, 2d ed. (Dallas: Word Publishing Company, 1990; reprint, Louisville, KY: Westminster John Knox Press, 1997), 16–30.

16. Ibid., 16.

17. No major commentators dispute that the image of God is equally shared by both sexes, although some authors, such as Gilbert Bilezikian, argue as if there is a major debate. See Jr. Raymond C. Ortlund, "Male-Female Equality and Male Headship: Genesis 1–3," in *Recovering Biblical Manhood & Womanhood: A Response to Evangelical Feminism*, ed. John Piper and Wayne Grudem (Wheaton, IL: Crossway Books, 1991), 97–8.

18. Helmut Thielicke, *Sex*, vol. 3, in *Theological Ethics*, trans. John W. Doberstein (Philadelphia: Fortress Press, 1975; Grand Rapids: William B. Eerdmans Publishing Company, 1979), 21.

19. Ibid.

20. Ibid., 22.

21. Lewis B. Smedes, *Sex for Christians: The Limits and Liberties of Sexual Living*, Rev. ed. (1976; reprint, Grand Rapids: William B. Eerdmans Publishing Company, 1994), 93.

22. Thielicke, *Theological Ethics*, 21.

23. John Murray, *Principles of Conduct: Aspects of Biblical Ethics*, 2d ed. (Grand Rapids: William B. Eerdmans Publishing Company, 1994), 29.

24. For a discussion regarding these orders, see Kaiser Jr., *Toward Old Testament Ethics*, 153; Barth, *Ethics*, 208–257; and Carl F. H. Henry, *Christian*

Personal Ethics (Grand Rapids: William B. Eerdmans Publishing Company, 1957), 242–245.

25. Grenz, *Sexual Ethics*, 32.

26. Kaiser, *Toward Old Testament Ethics*, 181.

27. Gilbert Meilaender, "The First of Institutions," *Pro Eccleisa* 6, no. Fall (1997): 448.

28. Some theologians today are claiming that the equality of the sexes necessitates that there be no differences other than biological ones. Some even deny biological differences. Both views, however, fail to understand that equality is not defined by sameness.

29. Though it is not the topic of the present study, various moral questions spring from this topic. For example, is it morally permissible for couples to use birth control? If so, what moral boundaries surround the use of birth control? Are couples permitted to use contraception indefinitely? How has the fall affected what God originally intended for couples regarding physical fruitfulness? What is the purpose of sexual intimacy? See Henry, *Christian Personal Ethics*, 243–244 for an interesting discussion of God's intentions for sex.

30. Martin Luther, "A Sermon on the Estate of Marriage (1519)," in *Martin Luther's Basic Theological Writings*, ed. Timothy F. Lull (Minneapolis: Fortress Press, 1989), 635.

31. Luther, "Estate of Marriage," 46.

32. Ibid.

33. Andreas Kostenberger, "Marriage and Family in the New Testament," in *Marriage and Family in the Ancient World*, ed. Ken Campbell (England: InterVarsity Press, in preparation). I used material from this work in its unpublished format, pages 19–22.

34. Ibid., 19.

35. Ibid., 21–2.

36. For an excellent discussion of the divorce debate see Gordon J. Wenham and William E. Heth, *Jesus and Divorce* (London: Hodder and Stoughton, 1984; reprint, Carlisle, CA: Paternoster Press, 1997).

37. Marriage, while intended to be life-long, is not eternal. In Matthew 22 Christ makes clear that in heaven, individuals will neither marry nor be given in marriage.

38. D. A. Carson, *The Sermon on the Mount: An Evangelical Exposition of Matthew 5–7.* (1978; reprint, Grand Rapids: Baker Book House, 1982), 45–46.

39. John Calvin, trans. John Owen, vol. 5, *Commentaries on the Twelve Minor Prophets: Zechariah and Malachi* (Grand Rapids: William B. Eerdmans Publishing Company, 1950), 552–3.

40. Paul Ramsey, *Basic Christian Ethics* (1950; reprint, Louisville: Westminster, 1993), 71–2.

41. "Of this alone even God is deprived—The power of making undone those things that have been done." *Nicomachean Ethics*, VI, 2,6:

42. "God cannot make what is past not to have been." *Summa contra Gentiles*, II, 25. See J. R. Lucas, "The *Vinculum Conguale*: a Moral Reality" *Theology* 78 (1975): 226.

43. E Schillebeeckx, *Marriage: Secular Reality and Saving Mystery* (London: Sheed and Ward, 1965), 203.

44. By 'can' we mean 'logically possible.'

45. See J. R. Lucas, "The *Vinculum Conjugale*: A Moral Reality," *Theology* 78 (1975): 226–30; and John Macquarrie, "The Nature of the Marriage Bond," *Theology* 78 (1975): 230–36.

46. Although I recognize some objections to the life-long nature of marriage being advocated in this study may arise from 1 Cor 7 and the "Pauline privilege," I will not be addressing those concerns directly. Because the focus of this study is covenantal nature of marriage in creation, I have limited, as all books must to some degree do, my discussions in the New Testament to those passages which deal directly with marriage and its creation in Gen 2.

47. R. Yaron, "The Restoration of Marriage," *Journal of Jewish Studies* 17 (1966): 5. Yaron also notes that the primary deterrent for divorce was financial, since the husband would be required to repay the dowry, as well as make a divorce payment.

48. Ibid., 8.

49. Ibid., 9.

50. Gordon J. Wenham and William E. Heth, *Jesus and Divorce* (London: Hodder and Stoughton, 1984; reprint, Carlisle, CA: Paternoster Press, 1997), 109.

51. Gordon J. Wenham, "Restoration of Marriage Reconsidered," *Journal of Jewish Studies* 30 (1979): 38.

52. Ibid., 39.

53. Ibid.

54. Cassuto, *From Adam to Noah*, 137.

55. David J. Atkinson, *The Message of Genesis 1–11*, The Bible Speaks Today, no. 1, ed. J. A. Motyer and John R. W. Stott (Downers Grove, IL: InterVarsity Press, 1990), 75.

56. See Abel Isaksson, *Marriage and Ministry in the New Temple: A Study with Special Reference to Mt. 19:13–12 (Sic) and 1. Cor. 11:13–16* (Copenhagen: C. W. K. Gleerup Lund, 1965), 23.

57. Ibid.

58. Ibid., 25.

59. In his discussion of the relationship between Jeremiah 3:1 and Deuteronomy 24:1–4, Fishbane argues that the grounds for divorce must be sexual in nature. See Michael Fishbane, *Biblical Interpretation in Ancient Israel* (Oxford: Clarendon Press, 1985), 308–9. "For, though the precise legal contours of the operative clause עֶרְוַת דָּבָר in Deut. 24:1 is a famous interpretative crux, there is little doubt that it carries a clear sexual component."

60. Noah Lathrop, "The Holy Scriptures and Divorce," *Bibliotheca Sacra* 56 (1899); J. Dwight Pentecost, *The Words and Works of Jesus Christ: A Study of the Life of Christ* (Grand Rapids: Zondervan Publishing House, 1981), 354–8;

and Isaksson, *Marriage and Ministry in the New Temple*, 139–42. For other proponents of this view, see Wenham and Heth, *Jesus and Divorce*, 279, note 7.

61. Marcus Cohn, "Betrothal," in *The Universal Jewish Encyclopedia: An Authoritative and Popular Presentation of Jews and Judaism Since the Earliest Times*, ed. Isaac Landman (New York: Universal Jewish Encyclopedia Company, 1940), 255.

62. M. Mielziner, *The Jewish Law or Marriage and Divorce in Ancient and Modern Times and Its Relations to the Law of the State* (Cincinnati: Bloch Publishing and Printing Company, 1884), 76.

63. Ibid., 82.

64. In addition to the five views cited in the following paragraphs, an additional argument could be used to support the life-long nature of marriage: the clarification view. According to this position, Christ gave no grounds for divorce but merely clarified whose actions caused the adultery. This position will not be evaluated because of its lack of biblical and scholarly support. See John S. Feinberg and Paul D. Feinberg, *Ethics for a Brave New World* (Wheaton: Crossway Books, 1993), 307; and Bruce Vawter, "The Divorce Clauses in Mt 5:32 and 19:9," *Catholic Biblical Quarterly* 16 (1954): 162.

65. Ibid., 160. Vawter himself does not hold to the inclusivist view. Rather, he is presenting the position of M. Brunec, "Tertio de clausulis divortii," *VD* 27 (1949): 10.

66. Ibid.

67. Ibid., 164. Augustine also makes this argument in *De conjugiis adulterinis* I, 9; PL 40, 456.

68. Ibid., 166.

69. According to the preteritive view, the two exception clauses (παρεκτὸς λόγου πορνείας and μὴ ἐπὶ πορνείᾳ) are allusions to the עֶרְוַת דָּבָר in Deuteronomy 24.

70. See discussion in J. Carl Laney, *The Divorce Myth* (Minneapolis: Bethany House Publishers, 1981), 70–1.

71. See William F. Luck, *Divorce and Remarriage: Recovering the Biblical View* (San Francisco: Harper and Row Publishers, 1987), 96–7.

72. Some theologians refer to this view as the "Rabbinic Interpretation," due to the prestige this opinion receives by support from Rabbis Bonsirven, Dollinger, Schegg, Patrizi, Aberle, Cornely, Prat, and Durand. See discussion in Vawter, "The Divorce Clauses" 162. Some recent supporters of this view include W. K. Lowther Clarke, *New Testament Problems* (New York: Macmillan Press, 1929), 59–69; W. K. Lowther Clarke "The Exceptive Clause in St. Matthew," *Theology* 15 (1927): 161–62; and Charles C. Ryrie, *The Role of Women in the Church* (Chicago: Moody Press, 1970), 40–50. Also, because it deals with lines of consanguinity and affinity, it may be called the "incestuous view:" see Feinberg, *Ethics for a Brave New World*, 307.

73. F. F. Bruce, *Commentary on the Book of The Acts*, The New International Commentary on the New Testament, ed. Ned B. Stonehouse (Grand Rapids: William B. Eerdmans Publishing Company, 1973), 315.

74. J. A. Fitzmyer, "The Matthean Divorce Texts and Some New Palestinian Evidence," *Theological Studies* 37 (1976): 209.

75. John Montgomery Boice, *The Sermon on the Mount* (Grand Rapids: Zondervan, 1972), 134–141; Boice, "The Biblical View of Divorce." *Eternity* (Dec. 1970): 19–21; J. Bonsirven, *Le divorce dans le Nouveau Testament* (Paris: Desclee, 1948); Paul B. Bull, *Marriage and Divorce*. London: SPCK, 1924, pp.7–9; Chase, Frederic Henry Chase, *What Did Christ Teach about Divorce?* (London: SPCK,1921), pp.27–28; Colblentz, John Colblentz, *What the Bible Says About Marriage, Divorce, and Remarriag* (Harisonburg, VA: Christian Light Publications, 1992), 21, 33–38.Von Dollinger, Johann Von Dollinger and Joseph Ignaz, *The First Age of Christianity and the Church*, trans. by Henry Nutcombe Oxenham (London: Allen & Co., 1866); Dirk E.T. Evenhuis, *Holy Matrimony*. (Smithton ,Australia: Circular Head Chronicle, 1997); William Fisher-Hunter, *The Divorce Problem* (Waynesboro, PA: MacNeish, 1952), 169–170; Anton Fridrichsen, "Excepta fornicationis causa" in *Svensk Exegetisk Arsbok* 9 (1944):54–58; Mark Gerald, "Jesus' Teaching on Divorce: Thoughts on the meaning of Porneia in Matthew 5:32 and 19:9." *Churchman* 92, no. 2 (1978): 134–43; Stephen Geise, "Until Death Do Us Part" http://www.geocities.com/sdgiesedts2001/DivorceTP.htm. Accessed 23 March 2004; Bill Gothard, *Supplementary Alumni Book*.Vol.5 (Institiute in Basic Youth Conflicts,1978–9), 9; Frederick Grant, "Marriage: The Gospel and the Canon." *The Churchman* (Sept. 1, 1937); Frederick C. Grant, *The Gospels: Their Origin and Growth* (London: Faber & Faber, 1959), 142; Frederick Grant, *The Gospel of Matthew*, Ch 1–13:52: *In the King James Version with Introduction and Critical Notes*. Vol. 1 (London: Eyre and Spottiswoode, 1955), 35; Dana Hartong, "Count the Cost."http://www.marriagedivorce.com/hartong.htm. Accessed 26 March 2004; Daniel Heimbach, *True Sexual Morality and Its Counterfiets: Biblical Standards at the Flash Point of Cultural Crisis* (*W*heaton, IL. Crossway, 2004); Abel Isaksson, *Marriage and Ministry in the New Temple* (Lund, Sweden: C.W.K. Gleerup, 1965); Brian C. Labosier, "Matthew's Exception Clause in the Light of Canonical Criticism: A Case Study in Hermenueutics." Ph.D. diss., (Westminster Theological Seminary, 1990); Noah Lathrop, "The Holy Scriptures and Divorce:*Bibliotheca Sacra* 56 (April 1899):266– 277; Johann David Michaelis, *Mosaisches Recht* (Frankfurt am Mayn: Johann Gottlieb Garbe, 1770–75); H.E.G. Paulus, *Philogisch-kritischer und historischer commentar uber das Neue Testamenti* (Lubeck: J.F.Bohn, 1804); Dwight Pentacost, *The Words and Works of Jesus Christ: A Study of the Life of Christ* (Grand Rapids:Zondervan, 1981), 354–358; John Piper "Divorce and Remarriage: A Position Paper." http://www.desiringgod.org/library/topics/divorce_remarriage/div_rem_paper.html.Accessed 23 March 2004.

76. See the above discussion of Deuteronomy 24:1–4 for why the "uncleanness" cannot be adultery or fornication.

77. *Gittin*, 90a. See Isodore Epstein, ed. *The Babylonian Talmud: Seder Nashim*, trans. Simon, Maurice (London: Soncino Press, 1936), vol. 3.7, *Gittin*, by Simon, Maurice, 436.

78. *Gittin*, 90a. For other discussions concerning the schools of Shammai and Hillel, see David Smith, *The Days of His Flesh: The Earthly Life of Our Lord and Saviour Jesus Christ* (London: Hodder and Stouighton, 1907), 355; Isaksson, *Marriage and Ministry in the New Temple*, 44–5; and J. W. Shepard, *The Christ of the Gospels: An Exegetical Study* (Grand Rapids: William B. Eerdmans Publishing Company, 1939), 452 who includes among the reasons given by the school of Hillel for divorce, "going in public with uncovered head, entering into conversation with other men, speaking disrespectfully of the husband's parents in his presence, burning the bread, being quarrelsome, or troublesome, getting a bad reputation or being childless (for ten years)."

79. See Pentecost's discussion of the betrothal view in Pentecost, *The Words and Works of Christ*, 356.

80. For a discussion of why πορνεία cannot be equated with μοιχεία, see Isaksson, *Marriage and Ministry in the New Temple*, 131–8.

81. See Lathrop, "The Holy Scriptures and Divorce" 270–71. Isaksson writes the punishment prescribed by Deuteronmy 22:20–21 was not practiced during the period when Christ was born, citing the *Ketuvoth*, a rabbinic tractate concerned with the question of marriage: Isaksson, *Marriage and Ministry in the New Temple*, 135.

82. By equating Jesus' use of πορνεία with "uncleanness" in Deut 24:1, the question arises: Does this not mean that "uncleanness" is sexual in nature, which contradicts earlier statements according to the betrothal argument. While the betrothal argument contends that "uncleanness" in Duet 24:1 cannot be adultery or fornication, both of which carried the penalty of death (Deut 22:20-22), this does not mean necessarily that the "uncleanness" could not be *any* form of sexual unchastity. For a discussion of the non-sexual nature of "uncleanness," see C. F. Keil and F. Delitzsch, *The Pentateuch*, Biblical Commentary on the Old Testament, no. 3, trans. James Martin (Grand Rapids: William B. Eerdmans Publishing Company, 1971), 417: "Adultery, to which some of the Rabbins would restrict the expression, is certainly not to be thought of, because this was to be punished by death." See also Ian Cairns, *Word and Presence: A Commentary on the Book of Deuteronomy*, International Theological Commentary, ed. Gredrick Carlson Holmgren and A. E. Knight (Grand Rapids: William B. Eerdmans Publishing Company, 1992), 211: "That [uncleanness] is not a case of sexual misdemeanor is clear from 22:20-22: the penalty for that is not divorce but death."

83. See discussion of the disciples' reaction in Pentecost, *The Words and Works of Christ*, 358. In response to the surprise of the disciples, Jesus taught marriage was not an option for everyone. Indeed, "There are eunuchs who were born thus from their mother's womb, and there are eunuchs who were made

eunuchs by men, and there are eunuchs who have made themselves eunuchs for the kingdom of heaven's sake" (Matt 19:12).

84. Although I am arguing for the indissolubility of marriage based upon its covenant nature, I acknowledge that a number of evangelicals recognize exceptions for divorce in the case of adultery or spousal desertion, exceptions which are incompatible with the covenant model advocated in this study. For example, G. Campbell Morgan writes, "So far as I am concerned, however, I am perfectly clear in my conviction that in the case of divorce on the ground of fornication the innocent party is absolutely free to marry again. I should have no hesitation in conducting the marriage service for such a one." G. Campbell Morgan, *This Was His Faith* (Westwood: Revell Books, 1952), 294. See also Leon Morris, *The Gospel According to Matthew* (Grand Rapids: William B. Eerdmans Publishing Company, 1992), 483; and John MacArthur, *The MacArthur New Testament Commentary, Matthew 16-23* (Chicago: Moody Press, 1988), 168–72.

85. Dennis J. McCarthy, *Old Testament Covenant: A Survey of Current Opinions* (Richmond, VA: John Knox Press, 1972), 3.

86. Hugenberger, *Marriage as a Covenant*, 182.

87. A similar implication may be suggested by Malachi's identification of the wife as "your companion" or "partner" 2:14.

88. Alice P. Mathews and M. Gay Hubbard, *Marriage Made in Eden* (Grand Rapids: Baker Books, 2004), 19–20. For a detailed discussion of this book, see my "A Response to *Marriage Made in Eden: A Pre-Modern Perspective for a Post-Christian World*." In *Journal for Biblical Manhood and Womanhood* 9, no. 2 (Fall 2004): 42–48.

89. Ibid., 171.

90. Ibid., 179.

91. Ibid., 184.

92. Ibid., 200.

93. Ibid., 206.

94. Ibid., 209.

95. Ibid., 280.

96. Ibid., 209.

97. See Daniel Doriani, "The Historical Novelty of Egalitarian Interpretations of Ephesians 5:21–22" in *Biblical Foundations for Manhood and Womanhood*, ed. Wayne Grudem (Wheaton: Crossway Books, 2002), 203–20.

98. See Wayne Grudem, "The Myth of Mutual Submission as Interpretation of Ephesians 5:21" in *Biblical Foundations for Manhood and Womanhood*, ed. Wayne Grudem (Wheaton: Crossway, 2002), 221–32.

99. Barth, *Ethics*, 235.

Index